# Kazan on Kazan

Michel Ciment

The Viking Press
New York

The Cinema One series is published by
The Viking Press in association with
*Sight and Sound* and the Education
Department of the British Film Institute

Published in 1974 in a hardbound and paperbound
edition by
The Viking Press, Inc.,
625 Madison Avenue, New York, N.Y. 10022

SBN 670–41187–6 (hardbound)
SBN 670–01974–7 (paperbound)

Library of Congress catalog card number: 73–11978

Printed and bound in Great Britain

# Contents

Cover: *America America*: the first view of a new land

44137

# Foreword

Loaded with critical praise and Academy Awards in the late forties and early fifties, Elia Kazan's films have since suffered a considerable neglect in his own country at a time when they revealed their author as a major artist. If Griffith and Ford are the ultimate references of the classical Hollywood cinema, it can be contended that Welles in the forties and Kazan in the fifties have been the most important disruptive forces in the modern American cinema. Few directors of the younger generation would deny Kazan's influence on their work. Through his direction of actors, his handling of contemporary themes, his obstinate progress towards independent production and the writing of his own work, he has set standards for personal creativity. The shape of this book has been dictated by the nature of Kazan's *œuvre*. His films are so closely linked to his personal evolution and to the history of his country – the interrelationship of the individual and the collective being in fact one of their main characteristics – that it seemed sensible to adopt the chronological order as a basic thread to follow his development.

By putting a particular emphasis on Kazan's more recent films, from *Splendor in the Grass* and *Wild River*, to *America America* and *The Arrangement*, this book also wants to stress their importance. Recognised as major achievements by such directors as Chabrol and Truffaut, Godard and Rivette, not to speak of new filmmakers from Brazil, Poland, or Italy, they can now be seen clearly as the most accomplished works of a mature artist.

This series of taped interviews was conducted in Mr Kazan's country house in Sandy Hook (Connecticut), over a period of four

Marlon Brando, Thomas Hanley and Eva Marie Saint in *On the Waterfront* weeks in August 1971, with some material added in January 1972.

I wish to thank Mr Kazan for giving me his time and offering access to personal material for the preparation of the interviews. I also wish to thank Roger Tailleur, author of one of the best books ever written on a film director (*Elia Kazan*, Editions Seghers, Paris) and a sure guide into Kazan's territory, Mrs Jacqueline Fakinos who helped me considerably in the transcription of the text, Mr Olivier Eyquem who worked on the filmography and the bibliography, and Wesleyan University for the facilities it gave me. Also my wife Jeannine, who, after spending hours with me seeing and discussing Kazan's films, spent as many hours typing the manuscript. Her support was invaluable.

M. C.

# 1: From Turkey to Yale

KAZAN: The Anatolian Greeks are completely terrorised people. My father's family comes from the interior of Asia Minor, from a city called Kayseri, and they never forgot they were part of a minority. They were surrounded with periodic slaughters – or riots: the Turks would suddenly have a crisis and massacre a lot of Armenians, or they'd run wild and kill a lot of Greeks. The Greeks stayed in their houses. The fronts of the houses were almost barricaded, the windows shut with wooden shutters. One of the first memories I have is of sleeping in my grandmother's bed and my grandmother telling me stories about the massacre of the Armenians, and how she and my grandfather hid Armenians in the cellar of their home ... The Armenians were lustier, their history a much bolder, more rebellious one. The Greeks were crafty, they did not rebel and they did not get killed as much.

The Greeks in Kayseri spoke Greek in the house, but outside, in the market-place where the men worked and the women shopped, they spoke Turkish. I still speak both languages. In other words, I speak the language of the oppressed and the language of the oppressor equally well. I went back to Kayseri in 1960, when I was preparing *America America*. All the Greeks had been transported out of that part of the world after Kemal's victory in 1922 in Smyrna. The Turks showed me the ruins of my grandfather's house, and his well. I remember they went down with a little bucket and pulled up some water for me to drink, but I didn't, it was very white, very milky, and I was concerned that it might be contaminated. I left them some money to repair the well. They treated me with the

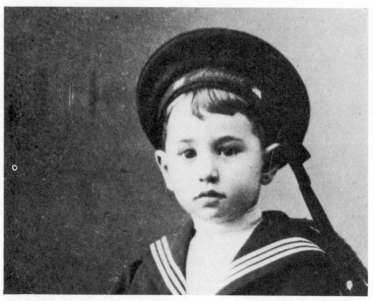

Kazan aged three – before emigrating to the States

greatest cordiality and friendship. I like Turkish people very much. But I think they had never allowed the Greeks to forget that they were a minority. On the other hand, the Greeks rather looked down on the Turks. They thought of them as beasts, animals without culture, without refinement, without gentility.

My mother was born in Istanbul as I was, but in a different suburb. Her family were cotton merchants. They imported from Manchester, England, and sold wholesale in Istanbul to various merchants, both Greek and Turkish, who took the goods out to the provinces. My mother's family was much better off, more cultured. Her brother was sent to school in Berlin. Her family lived in a much better house and they had servants. My father's people never had servants, and didn't read any book except the Bible in Turkish. Anyway, I was brought up in a family where both sides were aware that they survived by their wits, lived under constant threat. So when we came to America we brought with us the idea that we were still in a foreign country. I was four years old; we lived in a kind of Greek

10

ghetto in New York. My grandmother and my uncles and my parents lived in separate apartments in the same building and we always ate together on Sunday. We talked Greek and Turkish at home. We did not associate equally and freely with Americans.

My father traded in rugs. He was brought to this country by my uncle, who had a great deal of energy and cunning. They say the Jews have cunning, that they're sly people: the Anatolian Greeks are the same kind of people. If you want to know why: they couldn't protect themselves by force, by the sword or by arms, they were constantly being demeaned, so the only way they could get along was by being sly, by never saying the wrong thing. The first thing I learned was to shut up. My father used to tell us: 'Say nothing, don't mix in, don't mix in other people's business, stay out of trouble,' and that of course was the very opposite of the Yankee tradition. My first wife was a Yankee; her tradition was never to say anything except exactly what you felt and say it immediately without any omission or qualification. That's one of the reasons I admired and loved her so much: she was the opposite of the way I was brought up. But I was cautious and careful and crafty.

We lived on the West side, on 136th Street, between Broadway and Amsterdam Avenue. It was a lower middle-class neighbourhood. In the middle 1910s and the early 1920s, my father and my uncle were doing well. Oriental rugs were in vogue and they were able men in their field, good salesmen, they knew how to deal. At the age of five my mother sent me to a Montessori school. From the very beginning she tried to make me better than the society I'd come from. She gave me books, and got me to read.

CIMENT: *You were Greek, and Turkish and Orthodox; on top of that, you were educated in a Catholic school?*

My father always went to Greek church on Sunday. It drove me mad because the men always stand up in the Greek church for four hours. My mother read the Bible, but she was not a religious person in a ritualistic way: she did not go to church. Anyway, when I was about eight or nine, we moved to New Rochelle, N.Y., where we had a small house. My father, since there was no Greek church there, insisted I be brought up in a religion and sent me to a Roman Catholic Catechism School. I had a bad two years there. I was made to go to confession; I resented it.

In Greek families, we were brought up to be afraid of our parents, not to be loved by them or to love them, I mean our male parents, and we were brought up to stay home. I did not play with any children until I was eleven years old. I don't remember any single 'outside' person in my life until I was eleven. I did not play like a normal child would, I was kept segregated. It's the segregation a minority imposes on itself. I suppose it was meant to keep things pure, but really it was the result of terror, of fear. My uncles, who are nearly eighty, still don't mix with Americans.

*You went to Williams, a very Waspish college belonging to the Little Ivy League.*

This aggravated things in two ways. One was that my father was against my going there, and right after I went, it became clear I could not ask him for money. In 1929 the Depression came; he was hard up. So at Williams, after the middle of the first year, I was a dishwasher and a waiter. I was not invited to join a fraternity. I was what you would now call a freak, someone who is out of things. I only had two friends at Williams, so all my youth I was really closed off and friendless. I stayed in my room most of the time and read. At night I would go to work as a waiter. The boys did not feel friendly to me, or so I thought. I don't blame them now. I was not attractive, I would not respond in a normal way to anything they said. I was like a frozen wolf, very hostile.

I think the reason why I later joined the Communist Party and turned against everybody was born at Williams. I had this antagonism to privilege, to good looks, to Americans, to Wasps. I remember I served punch at the house parties and I saw these beautiful girls with these privileged boys. God! I would dream about them and think about them and masturbate. I never got any girl all that time I was in college. I thought I was very plain physically, I had pimples on my face. I had nothing to make me feel confident or secure. It's a sad story, pitiful in a silly sort of way, but it did hurt me, and it made me tougher. I think it gave me a lot of the qualities that made me persistent in my line of work, and tenacious. I think one of the good qualities I have is that I am very tenacious. I commit myself all the way as a person who wants to survive somehow, by any means! I always imagined society was hostile to me until quite recently; till I was almost fifty, I was not able to talk freely as I am talking to you now. I always felt if I revealed anything about myself I would be showing a weakness and through that hole I would be shot or destroyed.

At Williams I would make a lot out of little incidents. For example one day the boys started throwing rolls around, just good-natured fun. One of them hit me and I never forgot it. I never forgave them. I imagined they were throwing them at me; they were not, they were just throwing rolls around. My clothes always smelled of the dish-water; I made a big thing of that . . .

*The crash must have played an important role in your family life.*

It crushed my father. I have never portrayed it but I will in my next film and book. I remember vividly when the banks were closed. I remember all my father's friends and himself just sitting around their rug stores, with nobody coming in the door to buy rugs – week after week, month after month while their savings melted away. That's why Roosevelt was such a hero to these men – he finally got the economy rolling again.

I felt, yes, I felt they were getting what they deserved, the Americans, the rich Americans, the fraternity boys, the ones who left college and went right into a job on Wall Street. A lot of the best students in those days went right to Wall Street from Williams and immediately became involved with big companies, in favour jobs. I went out to nothing, I hadn't decided to be an actor yet. My father was urging me to go into the rug business but I could see that would collapse. I didn't like it anyway. I didn't like the dust and I didn't like the rugs. The whole thing about the Depression also led me into becoming left politically and I could see what the nature of the country was and I became in my twenties, mid-twenties, a sort of monster of hostility . . . I was ready then to play the leading role in *Waiting for Lefty*. I was full of anger, silent, unexpressed anger.

My last year at college I got good marks. I specialised in English and I had an English professor who introduced me to things like T. S. Eliot's *Waste Land*, and the novels of Frank Norris. In my last year in college I saw *Potemkin* for the first time, and I began to be interested in films. In those days there was no way to get a start in films. When I left college, I was looking for a way not to go into my father's business, a way to make my living in some way I respected. So I delayed and delayed just so I would not have to go to my father and say: 'I need a little money.' He wouldn't have given it to me anyway, because he didn't have any. By 1930 he was in very poor

13

shape and very demoralised. The Depression broke his back, just snapped his backbone like that, finished him.

I had to be on my own. But there was an opening at the Yale Drama School; one of my friends was going there and I went down with him. I could wash dishes in the cellar and get my food that way and then I could get free tuition because I tended the door and marked with little pins who came in and who went out. So between tuition and food I had about everything I wanted and I had a room there for two dollars a week. My mother used to steal a little money from her household accounts and send me a couple of dollars a week to pay for my rent.

At Yale I studied costuming, scenery, lighting, production. That was very useful for me because later I was never afraid of electricians, or scenic and costume people. No one thought I could act but they thought I could be a good builder of scenery, costume designer, an able production man backstage.

*Since you were so isolated, wasn't the Drama School contrary to your own tendencies?*

Yes, but it was full of freaks, oddballs. Strange girls, erratic boys ... I said to myself: 'Maybe I am in a zoo, but at least the animals are like myself, they are not the Williams men.' Even the teachers were nicer. They were freaks, too. There was one teacher there who was ready to leave the Drama School for an organisation I had never heard of, called the Group Theatre. He said to me: 'Why don't you come with me and be an apprentice with them?' To be an apprentice meant you waited on table. I waited on table seven years one way or another. But I was able to live that way.

*You wrote a lot of plays while you were a student.*

They were just one-act plays. I had a course with George Pierce Baker. He had been O'Neill's teacher and this was the very last year of his teaching life. He was an old homosexual, a fine old man. I got in his class and I wrote some plays. One of them, *Huge Cloudy Symbols*, was performed, twice on the same night, as a farce and as a serious drama. I didn't know it then, but this was an exact statement of the ambivalence within myself. Later in life, I tried to combine comedy and drama, feeling that things were both ridiculous and tragic at the same time. In that sense I'm an absurdist: I can take things tragically only up to a point.

14

# 2: The Thirties

When I entered the Group in 1932, three-quarters of the Group members were left-wing. The Group was the best thing professionally that ever happened to me. I met two wonderful men, Lee Strasberg and Harold Clurman, both of whom were around thirty years old. They were magnetic, fearless leaders. During the summer I was an apprentice, they were entertaining in a Jewish summer camp. They were paying their meals that way and I built and painted a lot of scenery for them. At the end of the summer they said to me: 'You may have talent for something, but it's certainly not acting.' So they told me to go elsewhere. I got a job in a play with the Theatre Guild as an assistant stage-manager, which is like third assistant director in films, running errands, giving cues, etc. But I was able to watch plays being rehearsed. It was at this time I got the idea: I don't want to be an actor, I want to be a director.

*While you were in the Group, you wrote two plays on strikes.*

One of these plays, *For Bread and Unity*, was about a bread strike. I was very much in the movement then. It expressed all the resentment I had accumulated all my life against the Turks, the American kids, Williams College, the fraternities, everybody. There was a committee within our little party cell; I was a leader of it in one sense, I was the one who went downtown and got orders on call there, urgent suggestions from 12th Street. One of the things the CP leaders always wanted to do was to get as much money as possible out of everybody. They were very short on money. The other thing they wanted was for us to take over the Group Theatre. The strike play was *de rigueur* at

15

that time; if you were in a theatre and could write anything, you wrote strike plays.

*There were interludes in the play, clippings, newsreels.*

I got that from Dos Passos. I thought his novel *USA* would be good in the theatre. Even then I was struggling for a way to keep the human drama in the social theatre. I did it through characters later, but what I was trying to say was: 'There is a social conflict going that influences and determines individual behaviour.' When I was first in the Communist Party I made speeches on a soap-box in Harlem on 116th Street with thirty people listening to me speaking against the government of Colonel Batista, against American involvement in Cuba. I did not speak very well ... Then I used to entertain a lot; in Union meetings I performed, with another communist, comic sketches, take-offs making fun of Hitler, of imperialism.

*The Soviet Union exercised a fantastic attraction in the thirties, not only politically but also artistically.*

There is no way for a man of your age to understand what that meant to us; we idealised the people in the USSR and what they did. And it lasted for ever. Even now, in a corner of my heart, when I hear someone say something bad about the Soviet Union, though I know it is reactionary there now and terroristic and backward and repressive – I knew this long before Krushchev's report – I knew it from the inside long before my testimony – despite that, to this day something clicks in me and I say: 'He should not say that, he should not think so.' One thing I admire about the young kids today is that they are so free to say that what they have in the USSR is reactionary. I idolised the Russians: we read that goddamn paper they put out for American consumption and we believed the lies they told. We adored their theatre: Meyerhold, Vakhtangov, Stanislavsky. We did imitations of their methods. I typed up Vakhtangov's notes and made a few carbons and gave them out to other members.

*In 1934 you staged your first play,* Dimitroff, *and worked on your first film,* Pie in the Sky.

Before *Pie in the Sky* I did a symbolic film with Ralph Steiner, an anti-war piece about two soldiers, *Café Universal.* Uprooted trees gave the idea that there had been a terrible battle many years ago.

16

The characters kept climbing mountains and falling off. Steiner directed it. He was a cameraman close to the Group Theatre. Then in the summer he and I did *Pie in the Sky*. It's about two tramps who go to a dump in Queens; they pretend for a day that they are orthodox priests, they take a tin can and put it on their head and then a long curtain or a rug and put it on their shoulders. It was a satire on all the orthodoxies. Ralph and I would discuss a scene, I'd set up the camera and then he would photograph it and I acted. In a sense I directed the performances and he directed the photography. It had the freedom that you can only get in partly improvised films. I never forgot that, the fact that on the location spot you can make up anything. We had a great time, as we did later while shooting *People of the Cumberland*. There we worked in the streets and everybody was so co-operative, except when they chased us from one city. This led me to feel later that my theatre education was against me in films: I often stayed too close to scripts.

*Dimitroff* was a carefully written play that used the words and the experience of Dimitroff in Germany in the Reichstag fire trial. In 1934 we decided to put on a programme of very left plays. We were already entertaining at unions (twice a week in my case) and on street-corners. The subject of this play was the burning of the Reichstag and Dimitroff's defence of himself against false accusations. Another fellow and I wrote this play, each writing scenes, then working together. *Dimitroff* is a very schematic play. It's hard to see now how anybody could have even liked it. It was poor, except that Dimitroff's words were ringing and he was played by J. Edward Bromberg, one of the leading actors in the Group at that time.

In the meantime Clifford Odets, to fill out the programme, wrote *Waiting for Lefty*, and his first idea was to make an outline of it and to have various writers of the Communist group to work on scenes. This was part of the plan to take the Group Theatre from Clurman and Strasberg and make it a Communist theatre. I was in *Dimitroff*, and also in *Waiting for Lefty* which was a big success and played constantly. I was the taxi-driver lifting my hands at the end and calling for a strike; the audience would yell 'Strike' back at me. We presented it downtown on a Sunday night and the roof fell in, the audience just went out of their minds. I guess it was the most exciting reaction I've ever seen in a theatre. It was fantastic, even more than

Kazan in the Group Theatre production of *Paradise Lost*

for *A Streetcar Named Desire*. People didn't leave the theatre, they stayed there for half an hour. And all around in the streets everybody was talking about it and yelling. This play and this feeling were the fruit of the Depression and we were determined that America would become socialised and change. Meantime our best friend Roosevelt was ruining our programme by making capitalism work!

*What was your experience as an actor?*

I worked like a maniac. First of all I took the Stanislavsky training with the utmost seriousness. I did all the physical work, gymnastics, acrobatics, dancing. I worked much harder than actors work today. I did sense-memory every day. You feel an orange and when you 'peel' it without touching it, you actually feel how the peeling feels to your fingers; I became very good at that. Then I took singing and speech lessons because I spoke like a New York street kid, very slangy. I thought of the roles mostly psychologically. I analysed the main drive of a character and from the main drive there were stems, the

18

'beats', that would build up the whole part. I understood how to divide a part into various tasks. I took innumerable notes, like I have all my life. But I was a very limited actor, I was intense, an intensity that came from all the pent-up anger in me. I didn't have much range. I was like an instrument with only three or four very strong notes. I was referred to in one review as 'the proletarian thunderbolt'. This kind of talent fitted the plays that Odets was writing. In *Paradise Lost* I played a gangster and in *Night Music* a resentful, dammed-up boy. In some peculiar and symbolic way the next step in the development of the 'proletarian thunderbolt' was to play gangsters in films. We used to say in the Communist Party that in American society you can either become a revolutionary or a gangster: both are bred by the same anger and the same resentment. The kids still say that you let your hostility out either in a creative way or in a destructive way. But there was a third possibility: to become an artist. The whole premise was that we were outcast, against the current of US life, and we thought that the revolutionary and the gangster had qualities that an artist needs in a hostile society.

But before we knew it we were with the current, we were not gangsters at all but valuable possessions for the motion picture studios. A lot of Group Theatre people like John Garfield, Franchot Tone, Bromberg, left for Hollywood. We looked down on them, we thought it was a defect of idealism on their part, that they were traitors. But when I look back on it, it is understandable that they would want this kind of security as they grew older, had children and other responsibilities.

*When did the Group Theatre first become successful?*

Not until *Men in White* directed by Strasberg at the beginning of its third year. It was the best play he ever did, directed in that peculiar, tense, internal way, but very effectively. Spiritually, it did not become a group until *Awake and Sing* by Odets, when the actors insisted that the play be done and there was a revolution against the leadership. Everybody's heart was in that play. In Odets' next play *Paradise Lost* we were still in the very heart of the Depression and we were working for whatever money came in. The top salary was 200 dollars but we were working on 80% cut, Odets included. I often got twelve dollars a week or eighteen. My wife was working in a department store and I used to work mornings in a store where I kept

Kazan (centre back with glasses) and Lee Strasberg (top right) with Group Theatre members

books for ten dollars a week. The only important thing in life was to keep the Group going.

*Wasn't the Group Theatre more timid, compared with the Theatre of Action and the League of Workers Theatre for which you also worked?*

No, I don't think so. More timid perhaps politically; but it was not timid in those days to walk a line left of centre and right of the Communist Party. The Group Theatre said that we shouldn't be committed to any fixed political programme set by other people outside the organisation. I was behaving treacherously to the Group when I met downtown at CP headquarters to decide among the Communists what we should do in the Group, and then come back and present a united front, pretending we had not been in caucus. The Theatre of Action was a collective and I lived there for a while. The Group was also a collective for seven or eight months. We all lived together, we all cooked, each person cooking one day a week. But in

20

the Theatre of Action and in the League of Workers Theatres, people were mean to each other. They were very narrow in their viewpoint, they had no breadth of artistic vision. In these groups the plays were typical Communist fairytales, wish dreams. Social iniquity would be solved by people getting together and performing a mass act. It didn't work that way in society, only on our stages.

*The Young Go First* was about the CCC (Civilian Conservation Corps): in Act I the unfairness to these youths who were working in the woods for the Roosevelt administration without salary would be shown. Then the kids would get together and decide on a programme. Then they would revolt. Then they would get some gains. Then there would be a last speech of determination to go on with the programme to further gains. It was a ritual, as unvarying as the Catholic mass. *The Crime*, which I also directed, was about the cohesiveness of a group led ideologically by a minority that prepared a social revolt. I had goons in the back, and they were shooting at the people on stage over the audience's head. I had all kinds of tricks like that, stolen from the Russian theatre. It was written by Michael Blankfort, who was a Communist then and later became President of the Screen Writers' Guild. Martin Ritt and Nicholas Ray were in it.

*What were your relations with the Federal Theatre?*

I worked there on a play called *The Revolt of the Beavers* – a play for children with exactly the same basic story as all the other Communist plays. A group of good beavers is being socially abused by an apparently stronger group. The abused group organises and revolts, wins minor gains, pledges itself to go on and win further gains. I did that while I was playing *Waiting for Lefty* and working as a stage manager on *Awake and Sing*. That was the end of my collaboration with the Federal Theatre. I was never influenced by it. I was influenced by three things: the Stanislavsky method as taught by Clurman and Strasberg, my readings of Vakhtangov, and films. I was very struck by *Potemkin* and Dovzhenko. I was influenced by my interest in American working-class life and the things I saw as I went around the country, the amount of colour and romance and excitement there was in the country.

*What kind of audience did you have in those theatres?*

In the Theatre of Action it was an audience of left groups, intellectuals like ourselves who aspired to be proletarian. It was not like

Germany; the workers did not come to attend our plays – they were at the movies. The Group Theatre had a middle-class audience – like us on the stage, though we wore taxi-drivers' caps. The ideas, the training, the taste were middle-class. Eisenstein, Pudovkin, Vakhtangov were also middle-class. You name me one proletarian artist!

*Then you left the Communist Party.*

I was tried by the Party and that was one of the reasons I became so embittered later. The trial was on the issue of my refusal to follow instructions that we should strike in the Group Theatre and insist that the membership have control of its organisation. I said it was an artistic organisation and I backed up Clurman and Strasberg who were not Communists. Everybody said I was a foreman type, that's the way they categorised things socially; I was in between the workers and the bosses. But it was a genuine conviction of mine because I thought very little of the artistic leadership abilities of my fellow-actors in the CP and nothing of their executive abilities. The trial left an indelible impression on me. It took place in Strasberg's house because his wife was a Communist then, and she asked her husband to leave for the evening. The chief speaker of the trial, the prosecutor, was a man I had never seen before. He was an organiser for the Automobile Workers Union in Detroit. He happened to be in New York then. He made a speech about the dangers of the foreman and, although he knew nothing about me, he damned me. I was the only one who voted for myself. Everybody else voted against me and they stigmatised me and condemned my acts and attitude. They were asking for confession and self-humbling. I went home that night and told my wife 'I am resigning'. But for years after I resigned, I was still faithful to their way of thinking. I still believed in it. But not in the American Communists. I used to make a difference and think: 'These people here are damned fools but in Russia they have got the real thing,' until I learned about the Stalin–Hitler pact and gave up on the USSR.

*At the same time* (*1937*) *you worked for Frontier Films on* People of the Cumberland. *The links between cinema and theatre were very close.*

I diffused my energy a lot. I worked in an organisation called

Kazan (centre) and Ralph Steiner (behind camera) co-directing *People of the Cumberland*

Frontier Films with Leo Hurwitz and a wonderful photographer, Paul Strand. The films that were made there showed the developing social conflicts in American society. I made a film with Ralph Steiner about strip-mining, not so much about the actual process as about the people: we showed their folk arts and how nice they were. I got great confidence in my ability to go into an environment and get drama and colour and entertainment out of the most ordinary people. I was able to make them act and dance and that encouraged me later – even as early as *Boomerang* – to go into the streets and not use actors: very often later I did not use actors because of this early experience.

Before *People of the Cumberland* I was mostly a middle-class boy who aspired to be a member of the proletariat: that was the pure class, I thought, the class that could not be corrupted and would not waver from its line, the revolutionary class. I always wore rough clothes and I still do, like a lot of the kids now who wear working-class clothes. It was a way of turning off, disavowing the middle-class, of professing visually that you are ashamed of your middle-class heritage.

*Was this your first contact with the country?*

It was my first contact as someone who worked in it. But from the time I left college I used to hitch-hike everywhere in the country because I was never comfortable at home with my father.

I had also become friendly with Communist organisers in the South, especially one who was living in Chattanooga, Tennessee, which is not far from where *Wild River* was made later. I went down to Tennessee often, just to be in his company, to study the situation and the social conditions. The revolutionaries today also go here and there wherever the action is. I used to do stuff like that even after I left the Party.

*You also worked on the radio at that time.*

I worked with Orson Welles who had a programme called 'The Shadow'. Around 1939, he would use me from time to time to play a gangster. He was a great swashbuckler in those days. He used to come into the studio as though he had been out all night. His valet brought a little suitcase with a fresh shirt, a fresh tie, and barber's stuff. While he was rehearsing, he would dress freshly and be ready to go on for the day. I admired that easy way of living. He was a terrific 'ham', and made deep and terrifying sounds with his voice. At the Group, we thought very little of him. To my mind the main influence on Welles is the technique of radio production. His films are very interesting visually but constructed aurally. I think they are not deep, in the sense that what they don't perceive is depths below the surface. But he has great theatricality. I like Orson a lot, but I wasn't influenced by him. I don't think he influenced anybody – he left nothing behind.

*In the late thirties you also made several trips to Hollywood.*

In 1936 I went there. A fellow working for Walter Wanger, Jack Wildberg, thought it was a good idea to put the Group Theatre people under contract. I was under contract for 200 dollars a week, which was pennies for Hollywood but a fortune for me. For a time I was going to be cast in *Dead End* in the part Allen Jenkins later played. But I made a test and they decided against me.

Kazan, Art Smith, Luther Adler and Bobby Lewis in the Group Theatre production of *Golden Boy*

*When you arrived in Hollywood somebody wanted to change your name?*

One day Wanger said to me: 'My God, you can't go into the movies with a name like Ee-*li*-a *Kay*-zan. That's impossible. I have a fellow who's an expert on names, I want to send you up to him.' So he sent me up to this guy's office. He said: 'What's your name?' I told him, and he said: 'My God!' Then suddenly he had an inspiration: 'Cézanne. *Cézanne!*' I said: 'Mr Horn, that's the name of a famous painter.' He said: 'Listen, you make a couple of pictures and they never will have heard of him.' He looked through the phone book for a first name; he said: 'We gotta give you an American first name to go with that.' He thought of Elliot – Elliot Cézanne. Then they asked me to have my nose operated on. I didn't do that, and I didn't change my name. I stayed there for seven or eight weeks and went back home.

*There were two trends in the thirties: Stylistic Agitprop and Realism.*

25

*You later tried in films to combine the two, to be true-to-life but also to get meaning from the story, not just copy it.*

The whole idea of the Group Theatre was to get poetry out of the common things of life. That was fired up by the Depression and our reaction to it. We felt that the whole basis of society had to be changed. Then there was another element: the Stanislavsky system made us see more in the lives of human beings, and it became our mission to reveal greater depths. Also, at that time, Freud had become popularised. All these trends came together in the Group Theatre: the political Left, the introduction to Freud and Marx, the absolute, idealistic dedication and determination towards a new world. As this failed, or collapsed, or didn't come off as quickly as we wanted, I think something more mature happened; we said: 'It will happen in time, we will still work for it.' I'm a child of the thirties. There's still something in me of the thirties which says, 'There will be a better world some day. We are going through a terrible struggle now, but it's not for ever and it's not inevitable.' I believe what Tennessee Williams does not. Williams is a child of the forties. I believe the world is getting better; I believe that people change for the better. That's why my hero, among American politicians, is Roosevelt. Some way or another, I believe in the existence of progress.

*Around 1938 you wrote an untitled play with Clifford Odets.*

One reason why the Group Theatre was collapsing, we thought, was that there were no plays. So Odets and I thought we were going to save the Group Theatre – it meant a lot to us, it was a spiritual home. After all, we thought we could write in no time one of those Broadway plays by George Kaufman or Moss Hart. We stayed one week in his room and what came out was not any good and we never did it. In 1938, the same year, I also wrote a thirty-page treatment for a movie, *Dream on Wheels*, with Bonnen.

*Did the way you directed develop while you were in the Group Theatre?*

I directed *The Young Go First* much better than I did Robert Ardrey's plays later. One reason was that I was intimidated by stars like Charles Bickford, Morris Carnovsky, and Luther Adler. Also I had come into the Group as an apprentice and they didn't really accept me as a director. It was a very snobbish group with all kinds of internal dissensions. They didn't make my work easier or happier. They were also full of a sense of competitiveness: why should I direct, I was just a new kid. At the end of the thirties – in 1939 in effect and in 1940 in fact – the Group Theatre collapsed and this left a huge void in all our lives. To everybody that had been associated with it, everything else seemed inferior, diffuse, without purpose. We had been brought to life by a cause. When the cause disappeared, our lives suddenly seemed empty, and futile and rather meaningless. Everyone went his way . . .

# 3: The Forties: Broadway, Actors, and the Studio

The first good directing job I did in the theatre was outside the Group: it was *Café Crown*, which I directed rather well with a good sense of humour. Humour was something new for any Group Theatre member – we were not strong on it. From that, in 1941, I got an offer to direct *The Skin of Our Teeth* which changed my life. I was offered the play, then for a while it became possible that Orson Welles might direct and it was taken away from me. After Orson Welles fell through, I was put back into it. It was a big success and from then on I began to be the white-haired boy of Broadway and suddenly very much in demand. It did not stop for fifteen years. All during this time, although I was involved in the theatre successfully, my ambition was to become a film director. I had no thought of becoming a writer. I didn't direct a film till 1944, after four or five Broadway hits. At one time I had four plays on the stage at the same time. It was a good period, but I kept thinking: 'I must get into films.' I was seeing more and more films and thinking and reading about them.

*Did you have a choice of plays on Broadway?*

After *The Skin of Our Teeth* I was offered a lot of plays. And after *A Streetcar Named Desire* I was offered any play. From 1946 to 1960 when I quit, all the plays were offered to me, without exception. I did the ones I wanted. From 1944 on I directed films and I was leading a two-coast existence. I would be in New York doing a play and at the

Frederic March in Kazan's Broadway production of *The Skin of Our Teeth*

same time people would come from California to work on plans for the film I was going to make next.

*Before you worked on Broadway you thought of creating the Dollar Top Theatre.*

Dollar Top Theatre was an idea I had after the Group Theatre collapsed. In 1940 I was determined to go on with it. In 1940, the new rise after the Depression was beginning to be felt. But by the time we got the thing organised costs had risen, we couldn't run a Dollar Top Theatre. Furthermore, as happened to me several times in my life, right after I started it I became interested in something else. We worked on it, we sent our programmes, we got several plays, but we never had a really good play to do. By the time we got organised, the 'dollar top' idea was no longer feasible. That was with Robert Lewis, by the way, the guy who became the other teacher at the Actors Studio.

*Some of the plays you did in this period anticipated some of your later preoccupations in the movies.* Harriet *and* Deep are the Roots *are about the South.*

I found the South very dramatic. It was a place that I was not much acquainted with – so it was not deprived of its romance. I knew just enough about it to be able to imagine anything happening there. It was the way Shakespeare – if I may draw a parallel! – thought of Italy: he thought anything could happen in Venice or Padua and he could make things up down there because he was not tied down by realistic knowledge. The South was glamorous and violent for me. It was the old and the new culture coming into conflict directly. The old culture is like Europe in the nineteenth century and the new one is very hip and up-to-date. There are many things I like there. The violence, the girls, the blacks, the humour, the folk-song, the whole look of it. It just fascinated me. I think some of it got into *Deep are the Roots*, but much more in the movies I did later.

*How did you prepare the staging of these plays?*

I would always go to the environment and get the atmosphere. It was a good preparation for the movies. People didn't do that in the theatre then. Also I would prepare the play along my version of the Stanislavsky method, defining what we used to call the spine, the main line of intention, and then the subsidiary actions that come off it like ribs.

*What kind of experience was* It's Up to You?

All through the war, I thought I'd be drafted any minute. But because I had two children, it was postponed. I volunteered to work for the Department of Agriculture. And in 1942 I was asked by them to do something about rationing that could be shown around the country by local theatre groups. I got the idea of having a piece of film in it in which the actors on stage would be talking to themselves in films and so debating with themselves about rationing. It was rather effective. There was also some dancing. It was all mixed media, with 95% play. Helen Tamiris, the choreographer, played a sirloin steak! A silly thing really.

*Was* It's Up to You *influenced by* Triple A Plowed Under?

Oh, no doubt. We were all affected by that part of the Federal Theatre – what they called the 'living newspaper'. It affected everyone in the theatre, because we suddenly realised how dramatic facts are. Brecht later used statistics, technology and information about the operation of things. Steinbeck always did that in his books; he showed how motors were put together and taken apart, for example. That technique in the theatre, absolutely unrealistic, affected us all. I think it affected Arthur Miller in *Death of a Salesman*.

*You also directed several musicals.*

I felt that music was not present enough in the work I was doing. I had been brought up in a strictly realistic, strictly psychological theatre tradition where I didn't use what Vakhtangov or Meyerhold used: songs and dances. I determined to train myself to that, though I was well into my career at that time. I went to see the best musicals to find what I could learn. I didn't do too well at that job, but I think one lesson was that I felt freer with songs and music from then on, and understood something about them and it began to appear in films I did later. I worked with Michael Kidd, Agnes De Mille, and was impressed by them. I admired the dancers, I thought they had more discipline and were better trained than the singers. Also I had some training in dance myself. I appeared as a dancer in a couple of recitals, including one by Tamiris. There was a dance that dramatised a wheel turning and turning in a factory, and I was the hub! I also danced with Jerry Robbins in the thirties, when he was just a dancer, before he became famous. So I began to be free in my movements. On stage I choreographed scenes more than purely psychological directors do.

My interest in folk-song in theatrical production started with the musical I did, *Sing Out, Sweet Land* – this is where I met Burl Ives. I always had a lot of feeling about the American folk song. Woodie Guthrie, Leadbelly, had been friends of mine from the road and from the South. Later *Cat on a Hot Tin Roof* ended with a pantomime scene performed to the music of Sonny Terry and Brownie McGhee – a couple of black folk singers whom I was able to use that way because of my experience in this kind of music.

An important thing happened around 1945. Arthur Miller, who was just a young fellow beginning to write – he had written radio plays for the Theatre Guild – saw *Deep are the Roots* and was interested by my directing. He offered me his new play, *All My Sons*. We were immediately compatible in the sense that his background was very much like my own. His father was a salesman like mine, he came out of the lower middle-class like me, he was also from New York. We understood each other immediately. I was for a time the perfect director for him and this showed most in *Death of a Salesman*, which is a play that dealt with experiences I knew well in my own life.

But the playwright I found myself the furthest away from in material and closest to personally, and I can't tell you why except that I admired him so much, was Tennessee Williams. I felt very close to him. I thought he had genius. With Miller I could always see where he had derived his materials. Although I could see the excellence of what he did, I was never surprised. But with Williams there was always something that would startle me, there was always a new brilliant illumination. I was overwhelmed by Williams. At one time I would have directed anything he asked me to, and I did – I directed four plays of his.

Lee J. Cobb (second from right) in Kazan's stage production of *Death of a Salesman*

*Did the plays you directed in the early forties relate in any way to your future interests?*

To me, *Jakobowski and the Colonel, Dunnigan's Daughter, Harriet, The Skin of Our Teeth* were just technical jobs. I didn't begin to feel that the material of my own life could be dramatised before I read Arthur Miller's plays. Anything up to 1946 in the theatre and in films was done by a proficient, technical director, nothing more. With *Death of a Salesman* there was something added – which was: 'this is to some extent the story of my own life.' Around *Viva Zapata!*, I began to look purposely for material that was expressive of myself. *East of Eden* (1954) is a fable of my own relationship to my father. And of course *East of Eden* is much closer to me than *Death of a Salesman*.

On Broadway I directed Helen Hayes, Mary Martin, Tallulah Bankhead, who was a monster – I don't mean entirely bad, but bigger than life – Freddie March, his wife Florence Eldridge. I had to deal with stars who were often rather suspicious of me because they said: 'Yes, the young Stanislavsky is coming around and trying to tell us how we should act.' I had to put them at their ease, make them confident and still get good results from them. It was good training for me later to deal with every actor as a different and individual problem. It liberalised me instead of making me stricter and more ritualistic in my artistic approach. I developed a range – from the non-actor, such as I had in *People of the Cumberland*, to a very strict and rather ossified professional like Tallulah Bankhead who had only one way of performing.

In the Group Theatre we used to have long rehearsal periods and talk a lot. Well, if you talked with these actors I was working with on Broadway, then they became uncertain because they felt that you were showing off your intellectual gifts and thereby minimising their own. I found that with these people it was better to cajole them, to get them on the right track by the means that suited them. The danger in something as passionate and devoted as the Group Theatre is that you become insular, become a man with only one attack for technique. I got over it during those years.

*The Group Theatre broke with the English tradition in the American Theatre.*

It was exactly the opposite to the then British tradition. The then British tradition was an imitation of behaviour. That is, a person would study the external manifestations of a certain experience or emotion and imitate them. The Group actors would induce the actual emotion within themselves and then judge or try to control what came out of it. We would get ourselves *into* the state of the actor of the role rather than imitate the externals of the role. In that sense, we were diametric. More than that, the English acting of the twenties and the thirties imitated other performances so it was even once more removed. That's why the Group and the Actors' Studio had such an influence up to five or six years ago on the young British actors. Tony Richardson and the Royal Court were influenced by the production of *Streetcar* and *Death of a Salesman* and so was John Osborne. Their productions were also looking for a natural rather than a theatrical movement, for an ensemble rather than a star feeling, everything being subordinated to the projection of a theme

34

rather than entertainment. I think the Group Theatre was the greatest influence on the world theatre since the great Russians of the twenties.

*How did you direct plays in those days?*

I tried to put myself in the author's shoes. I used to try to say: 'I'm now speaking for this author.' Each author is different. I said to myself: 'I'm doing *Tea and Sympathy* by Robert Anderson – this should be like a Chopin prelude, light, delicate, without overstressing' or 'I'm doing a play by Tennessee Williams: he's morally ambivalent, he admires the people who destroy him, he doubts himself, he is afraid of certain people and yet he is drawn to them. I must see life like he sees it.' When I did a play by Arthur Miller, I said to myself: 'This man deals in ethical absolutes (at least he did through the plays I directed), he is absolutely certain where he stands on issues. He is certain maybe because he is afraid of facing ambivalences, but I must not introduce ambivalences. I must keep it clear, forceful. I must save up force for the last part because he makes a final summation statement at the end of every play.' And so on, and so on. In other words, I tried to think and feel like the author so that the play would be in the scale and in the mood, in the tempo and feeling of each writer. I tried to *be* the author, I was many men but none of them was myself. That's why I like my films so much more than I do my plays although I was accorded much more absolute praise when I did plays. My films are my own face, they have my faults and my characteristics.

*1947 was an important year: a play you directed won the Pulitzer Prize, you got the Academy Award for* Gentleman's Agreement *and you started the Actors' Studio. Was there an evolution in your ideas about acting between the end of the Group Theatre and the founding of the Actors' Studio, and why did you found it?*

The Group Theatre had meant a lot to me and I missed it personally and professionally. I missed the fact that there was training going on, that the tradition of the Group had stopped functioning. I missed it, not as a memory or as something of the past, but as a place where I could find new actors, where I could work myself on things of an experimental nature. I was right to miss it because out of the first classes of the Actors' Studio came people like Julie Harris, Karl Malden, Kim Hunter, Marlon Brando, Jimmy Dean, Pat Hingle, and so on. It was like a farm where I was raising new products that I would use, but also deeper than that: I'd started as an actor and my craft up to that time was based on acting. It was important to me that it be kept going. It was started as a small, modest group. There wasn't much to it, just two classes; I taught one and Bob Lewis the other. I said to myself: 'I have to make a whole generation of actors.' And we did that. I took the basic exercises of the Stanislavsky method – developing the senses, developing imagination, developing spontaneity, developing the force of the actor and, above all, arousing his emotional resources. I had taken those classes myself from Clurman and Strasberg in my time. I had taught downtown at the New Theatre League, the Communist Theatre. So I'd had quite a bit of experience teaching by then.

Everybody came to the doors of the Actors' Studio. I used to be one of the three judges, with Strasberg and Crawford; we used to judge the auditions of aspiring actors every two months or so. I used to know all the kids. They would perform a short scene from a play. We were always interested to see what plays they preferred. They varied through the years. At the beginning they were usually plays by Clifford Odets, then they became plays by Tennessee Williams and Arthur Miller, then five or six years later they were plays by Edward Albee and Harold Pinter. You could tell what was in young people's minds by the plays they submitted themselves in. I liked the Actors' Studio a lot. It had no goal except to give the actors a place to work. It gave a lot of people much happiness, much friendship, acceptance, a sense of being safe and wanted, and training. The actor's position in our theatre is a very bad one, very humiliating; what the Actors' Studio did just humanly was a wonderful thing.

This went on from about 1947, and I was satisfied with it, right through 1952, 1953, 1954 when I did *On the Waterfront*. I was teaching both classes then – I had the older class later. I tried to continue with these people. And I had people like Anthony Quinn, Rod Steiger, Marlon Brando, Shelley Winters – and whenever that cocker James Dean came around, I had him too. But I knew by this time that teaching was not for me, that I didn't have the patience or the stability for it. I liked that the Studio existed but I would shrink from totally committing myself to it. I liked to wander around the world and the country and do a lot of different things. The whole thing in my life then was multiplicity. Fifteen years later it became singleness, that is to write and film about the stuff that deeply interests me and has affected my life. Then I was both a free soul and wanted to be tied down and have a home. The Actors' Studio was my artistic home. It was also like a moral burden on me, in the sense that it was up to me to continue what the Group Theatre had given me.

So I was looking around for someone who was by nature a teacher, and I knew who I had in mind: Lee Strasberg. It took me a long time to get Strasberg involved; he hesitated, he backed off, he qualified, he did everything in the world to try and get out of it. I just persisted. About that time I was beginning to collaborate on the preparation of scripts like *Face in the Crowd*, *Splendor in the Grass*, and so on. I was directing plays and movies both, in those years; I didn't have time to go teach, and didn't have much interest in it after a while. I wasn't a particularly good teacher. I would be very good some days and then on other days I would find the work tedious and get through it as best I could. Strasberg − it fits him perfectly, he's a superb teacher. I think he's a very fine man. He's very criticised by many of my friends but I admire him a great deal. The Actors' Studio and he became synonymous, which is the way I wanted it. The Actors' Studio and this kind of acting have become the central tradition of American acting. Now, not only all these actors have become famous, but they have followers. I quit the Actors' Studio at a good time because it was becoming something I didn't want it to be. At a certain time, after Strasberg was in there and it became his place and not mine, I kept pulling back, and though he kept holding me over the years, slowly and slowly I withdrew. When I saw that he was happy there and comfortable and secure and wealthy, I left. He always wanted to make it a producing thing, to make a theatre of it. I was never interested in that idea. But as a training ground it was of great value.

*Your feeling for collaboration must come from the Group Theatre.*

There's a fundamental difference: I think there should be collaboration, but under my thumb! I think people should collaborate with *me*. I think any art is, finally, the expression of one maniac. That's me. I get people who help me, but I'm the centre of it. The whole damn thing in the Actors' Studio, by the time I left it, was that everybody had a voice, and everybody was equal, and everybody knew how they should do things. That's fine for a school, but it has nothing to do with art. Art is the overwhelmingly strong impression that one obsessed visionary puts on his work. It's important that the people who collaborate with you are able to see things as you do, but also that they're willing to ask you what you want and try to give it to you. When I have people I like, it's enormously pleasurable. And I like being contradicted because it helps the work, so long as I can, at a point, say; 'That's it.' But I think a lot of other directors don't allow contradiction because they're afraid. They're not certain enough of themselves. If you're certain of yourself, you can hear all the other voices; if you are not certain of yourself, you're anxious, and you don't want everybody to talk. If you don't let anybody express himself, that's bad too. With actors, I allow a tremendous amount of initiative. I always set the goal of each day first; I tell them what I want that day. The good actors have often surprised me by giving me my goal, my result, through means I didn't anticipate. That's the best way.

There's a period in the rehearsal of a play which hasn't quite got a parallel in a film: after you rehearse a play for about ten days or so, you begin to want something to happen against you. You want actors to take the play over, to make it theirs, to eliminate you. If you've rehearsed it well, the actors are on the track, and doing the things you want, but they've also pushed you to the back. In the first days of rehearsal you're up on the stage with the actors: by the end of the first week you sit in the first, second, or third row; about the tenth day you begin to move back; and in the second week you're sitting in the back row. You let them run without interjecting any criticism. After a play opened, I disappeared.

*Don't you think there was a particular kind of relationship between the Russian school of acting and some American trends?*

I think that Stanislavsky was particularly suited to be adopted by the American theatre. For instance, in Chekhov, whom he staged a lot, there is the use of silence, a surface realism and strong feelings working underneath, which is very close to O'Neill. And today the new directors on the stage oppose theatre to drama, theatre being the gestures, the silence, the choreography, etc., and drama being the written text. Before the Group, O'Neill brought in Freud, the interest in inner conflicts, the demon and the angel in the same person. Stanislavsky was also peculiarly suited to us because he emphasised not the heroic man but the hero in every man. That Russian idea of the profound soul of the inconspicuous person also fits the American temperament. We have not got the burden that everybody should be noble, or behave heroically, that the English used to have. We helped them get out of it.

*Why did you never stage O'Neill?*

Once I wanted to stage one of his plays and met him and he said he preferred an Irishman! and to myself I said: 'Fuck you! Get an Irishman' – and he did and the Irishman did very well! After his death I wanted to stage another play of his. But his wife preferred to give it to José Quintero, who is not Irish. It was *Long Day's Journey Into Night*, a beautiful play, and it was a huge success!

*Brecht criticised Stanislavsky's Method and psychoanalysis as having a common aim: to fight against a social illness without using social means so that only the results of the illness can be fought against but not the causes.*

A good remark. When I saw the productions that were made under his direct influence in East Berlin, I thought they were very well acted and didn't correspond, as I saw it, to his theories of alienation or removal. They were not cool. Where I felt he was true to his theories was in the scripts he wrote where he would constantly keep the social and political causes of things in the foreground so that you would understand not only the events but why the events came to be. Later I tried to emphasise that too. I didn't feel that his theories of acting were worth much, not that I was against what he did, but actually I didn't see him doing what he said he was going to do.

*For you the Method was not a theory but a practical objective.*

The Method is more than a system for actors. It is a method for training actors and not a few handy rules. This training leads to the second aspect which the Method represents – how to rehearse a play:

– there must be a permanent company that stays together with basic training and several productions,

– this company must be trained in the same way and have the same social and artistic ideals,
– the rehearsal of the play must take several months to do and be at one stage freely improvisational and at all times the work of an ensemble.

One aspect of the Method is a way of controlling and using the unconscious; so that things are not just impulsive, they must be structured. We were very oppressively aware in New York how unfortunate and quick our rehearsal period was. Most plays are rehearsed in two and a half weeks because the third week you are in the scenery. You are trying on costumes, you are not really rehearsing.

*Did you use the 'as if' method as a stimulus?*

That's not a way I like. It means that for instance when you talk to so-and-so it is as if you are talking to your mother and so on. At the beginning I used it because it is a neat, handy device. But the more genuine thing is the true situation. Many of these tricks were debasements of the Method, reducing it to a series of easy rules. Americans like handy rules, quick solutions.

The idea with the Method was to consider the play like the trunk of a tree with the branches coming out and you had a branch that led you to another branch and slowly you came to the first climax of the play which contained the theme. The idea was that if you performed all the tasks on the way you would be able to perform the task at the end. We used to refer to it as the spine with all the vertebrae coming off it. So when I was preparing films I also tried to capture in a phrase what the essential task was, to sum it up in one sentence.

The Method also gave me a way of getting the psychology clear, of charting the progress of a character through a film. Tennessee Williams did not agree with me – he said I was exaggerating, that it came from my Communist days when we thought people would become clearer and better with time. He thought people went on behaving the same way all their lives. He has a tragic view of life which is not mine; I would agree with him only in the sense that I believe our characters are our fates.

There's a basic element in the Stanislavsky system that has always helped me a lot in directing actors in the movies. The key word, if I had to pick one, is 'to want'. We used to say in the theatre: 'What are you on stage *for*? What do you walk on stage to get? What do you want?' I always asked that of actors; what they're in the scene to obtain, to achieve. The asset of that is that all my actors come on strong, they're all alive, they're all dynamic – no matter how quiet. The danger of the thing may be a frenzied feeling to my work, which is unrelieved and monotonous. In my later works I try to allow myself to rely more on quieter effects. Another thing in the Stanislavsky system that I always stress a lot when I direct actors is what happened just before the scene. I not only talk about it, I sometimes improvise it. By the time the scene starts, they're fully in it, not just saying lines they've been given. Sometimes I do a scene that's unrelated to the scene in the script, something that happened, say, a day before, but that motivates the scene, so the actor knows what he's bringing into the scene that he plays. All these things are cinematic in that they take the reliance off the dialogue, off the spoken word and put it on activity, inner activity, desire, objects, partners – partners being the people you play with. All this can be photographed: the movement to achieve something can be photographed, what you are trying to achieve – the object – can be photographed, the partner and your relationship to him can be photographed. The lines are put into what I think is their proper place, into a secondary position. That's more or less the way I try to work. Another thing I've tried to stress is a basic simplicity; that is, listening to the person who's talking to you, and talking to him, not declaiming. I initially and immediately try to break down any declamatory, old-fashioned theatrical remnants in the style of the performer. And very often, when I've worked with a performer and then I don't see him for a while, and he appears in someone else's picture, I realise he's gone back to over-theatricalism.

*How do you cast?*

The problem is that the basic channel of the role must flow through the actor. He has to have the role in him somewhere. He must have experienced it to some extent. That's why I don't cast by reading. I take the actor for a walk or I take him to dinner or I watch him when he doesn't notice it and I try to find what is inside him. I am known for casting 'on instinct', which is not the correct word because I have studied the actor carefully, even if quickly. Sometimes I make very rapid decisions but I never cast by looks because looks are false. And

41

I don't believe in heroes anyway, so good looks don't mean anything to me.

An actress who played a leading role in a play I cast because her husband, whom she had divorced, had told me all about her sex habits. She was a very proper girl when you looked at her but I knew what she really was, so that's how she got cast. I know a lot about the personal lives of actors. At the Actors' Studio I knew the actors not only as technicians but as people. The material of my profession is the lives the actors have led up till now.

*Because of Brando and Dean you are known more as a director of actors. But you also discovered many actresses and most of your female characters have a certain tenderness in common.*

I'm better with actresses. And I think your remark about the tenderness is true because for me it's part of sex. I like womanliness, I like character in a woman. I don't like little girls of thirty. My first wife was a strong person. And so is my second. I like in a woman what is primitive, elemental, which could make her kill somebody who broke in the house to threaten her children. I don't like the wishy-washy type. I like strong creatures like Lee Remick, Jo Van Fleet, or Barbara Loden. I admired my actresses. Women are an ideal to me, partly because of my mother. They are civilising, fair, staunch, undefeatable, encouraging. Men, with the exception of Clurman, Strasberg, and Lighton maybe, had much less influence on me.

*How do you rehearse?*

I slowly begin to rehearse the next scene without rehearsing it; I lead them up to it without saying: 'Now, let's siddown, come on, everybody.' I mean I don't act like a boss: we're collaborators. In their dressing-rooms, I start talking to them about the next scene, the moments in it, what happens in it, and what happens before it, particularly. It's very important, that you re-establish what happens before it. So before you know it, we're rehearsing. I've always got to have the actors ready at the same time the scenery's ready. If they can do their work and if they can be ready – so that when the crew sees, or the other actors see the scene, they see it in some sort of shape – they feel protected. If they know that I've approved of what they've done, they feel protected too. That's very important, to get them over their shyness and uncertainties, privately, before-hand.

Another thing I do is – I throw them little new problems as they go along – little changes – I revise the thing for them. A performance is like a little flame, it's about to go out, you throw some more kerosene or gasoline on it, so it comes up again. You know what the source of the scene is, in the actor, so you keep it revived by the little things you say.

*But did you change your way of handling actors between 1950 and 1970?*

I'm not as interested in the minutiae, in the small psychological turns, as I used to be – I'm interested in broader strokes now. I don't explain everything as I used to, I'm not psychologising so much. I used to direct so carefully that every little psychological turn and twist was important.

*Your actors used to be more flamboyant – it seems they're more relaxed now.*

Right, they're more relaxed, less showy, less affected. But what gets better now is my themes. They used to see my pictures and they'd say: 'Ah, what a great performance Karl Malden gives, wasn't Kim Hunter wonderful?' But the play or the film was a platform, where these set pieces, these showpieces were performed. Now I want the basic theme of the thing to come out.

I was also, in those days, in the theatre particularly, protecting scripts that I felt were weak. I avoid doing that now, I trust myself and the material more. I say that even if it's a little boring, even if it's a little slow, that's what I'm talking about. I don't want you to watch how flashy this performance is, I want you to think about what's really going on. Sometimes it's not even bad to do it that way – a little boring, a little slower – it's not bad. I never did it till about ten years ago. Somebody just sits on a porch, in the front yard there's a cow. Or Kirk Douglas' mother is just sitting with her hands folded in a hospital waiting-room, she doesn't move, she doesn't say anything, she's not crying, she's just sitting there and you feel – I photograph through a window – how lonely she is, right? She doesn't say: 'Oh God, I'm lonely!' Nothing. You let the audience work. That's another thing I'm still trying to learn, which is to let the audience feel, don't

tell the audience what they should feel, let them find it, trust them to. It took me many years to get this.

*How did you use objects to convey feelings?*

In *Wild River*, for instance, Clift is coming back to Lee Remick's house. It's raining, and Lee Remick has a towel in her hand. The inside of the house is warm. Whatever shyness she had, it'd be natural for her to welcome him into the house. But she's shy about touching him except for the towel. The towel is an excuse to touch him. If it were a nice day and he'd just come in, the scene would have been impossible. One of the basic things in the technique of the Method is to use objects a lot. All objects are symbols of one thing or another. It's something you can *see* move from one hand to another, you can see it break, or you can see it captured, you can see it sold, you can see it bought, you can see it transferred, you can see it embraced, you can see it thrown away. That's like making an act out of a feeling, through the object. Of course, it helps actors who are self-conscious, because if they concentrate on the object they won't be concentrating on themselves.

*The device of the swing in* Baby Doll, *that was also using an object and a movement . . .*

Right . . . She would allow things on the swing that she wouldn't elsewhere. Also, on the swing she can't walk away easily, all he's got to do is put his hand across her. Also, she's a baby girl, the swinging makes her more at ease. Also, there's something seductive about the movement itself. Also, he was *playing* with her. I had a wonderful mood in that picture of playfulness plus seriousness. You didn't know when he was serious or when he was playful. That's what Williams does so well – you don't know how far he means it and how far he's kidding about it, how far it's important to him, and how far it's just a tease, a joke.

There's another example of this use of objects in a scene that was partly accidental and partly the talent of the actor who was in it: that scene in *On the Waterfront* where Brando is walking Eva Marie Saint home, rather against her will; and she on the one hand is attracted to him, and on the other hand wishes that he'd leave her alone because there's a social stigma attached to him, so she'd rather lose him, and at the same time she's attracted to him and would rather keep him.

45

And he, too, is attracted to her, but he's also shy, and tense about connecting with her because he was responsible for the death of her brother. But mainly Brando wants to keep her, despite her desire to get rid of him. As they were walking along, she accidentally dropped her glove; and Brando picked the glove up; and by holding it, she couldn't get away – the glove was his way of holding her. Furthermore, whereas he couldn't, because of this tension about her brother being killed, demonstrate any sexual or loving feeling towards her, he could towards the glove. And he put his hand inside the glove, you remember, so that the glove was both his way of holding on to her against her will, and at the same time he was able to express, through the glove, something he couldn't express to her directly. So the object, in that sense, did it all.

There's another example in *East of Eden*: there's a scene where Dean takes his younger brother to see his mother, and he opens the door and shows the younger brother his mother – if you just did this with the feelings, with close-ups of the feelings, you would show Dean wanting to hurt this boy. So on Dean's face you would get something vague, which is, he wants to hurt his brother – and on his brother's face you'd see he gets hurt. But they'd look very much alike. When we tried to find an action that contained these emotions, and dramatised them, we found that Dean not only *showed* his brother his mother but he threw his brother at his mother. Now this was especially *à propos* because the brother was a puritan. So he says: 'Not only will I show you the shit that you come from, but I'll rub your face in the shit that you come from.'

*How did you win the confidence of actors?*

I remember rehearsing *Jakobowsky and the Colonel* – a whole week, it was terrible, just terrible. So I knew I was off; I was directing comedy as if it was drama, and it was awful! The actors were obeying everything I said, and they were like children. Then I learned a great thing: I went to the actors and I said: 'Look, I've directed this thing terribly. It's awful. Forgive me. We are going to start at the beginning. There's no use temporising or going halfway, we've got to throw away everything we've done.' And all said: 'Sure!' And from then on I never disguised my views or saved my pride. I'd tell them everything. They like it when you say you have difficulties, it makes them feel good. And you *do* have difficulties, everything isn't easy, it's hard. Sometimes you do a bit of work that's not so hot and you say, 'That's not very good, is it?' and they laugh and say, 'Well, he's very human.' Rather than keeping the style 'I know everything' – which was the way I was when I started.

*You certainly didn't believe realism to exist in the theatre – even in Tennessee Williams you had actors speaking to the audience.*

Well, I don't say it does not exist, but at its best today the theatre that is good is the theatre that says: 'This is a convention. So we speak to you the audience, we recognise your presence, we recognise that we're trying to affect you, and we do it in different ways.' I did that in *Cat on a Hot Tin Roof* and I think it was the first time that it had been done for many years. The last time it had been was about 1938, in *Our Town*: Thornton Wilder had a man on the side of the stage who spoke to the audience. My man didn't stand on the side, he walked right to the centre, all eyes on him, and he looked at the audience rather aggressively and threateningly, then he started to defend himself to them. It was very effective, it scared them, because he was a big male and they all liked it, fortunately.

*But in a sense, would you say that the natural outlet of the Method would be the cinema?*

There's a lot of truth in that, but I don't agree with it completely. The camera looks into the people, so the need for life to be there is important; but the wonderful thing about the movies is that there are so many other elements: the *plastic* elements, the dance, the movement, the *visual* elements, the composition, the *oral* elements, the music of city sounds, of country sounds. And the element of nature, the effect of nature on experience, the relationship between the experience and the act, the experience and the environment, the wind, rain and snow, dawn and dusk, the whole thing!

*What was your problem in using the Method in films?*

Everybody's problem is his talent, not his faults. My problem is that I can always make things forceful. I used to make every scene GO GO GO! mounting to a climax, and if I had sixty minutes in a picture there were sixty climaxes, *ready? CLIMAX! all right, rest a minute – CLIMAX!* That was what I used to do. And it's easy to do, you know, make somebody shout, or grab somebody by the neck or throw somebody out, or slam a door, or open a window, or hit somebody with a hammer, or eat something quick in disgust — it's easy to do. It's bullshit! Bullshit! So you see what I mean, the problem of a man is his virtues, not his faults. It was my facility, my experience, my knowledgeability I had to watch out for.

# 4: The Forties: the Films at Fox

*How did you come to work in Hollywood?*

In 1944 I began to get offers from the companies, particularly
Warners and Fox, both of whom did more contemporary, down-to-
earth subjects. I was offered *A Tree Grows in Brooklyn* and *A Letter
to Uncle* by Clifford Odets. Jerry Wald wanted me at Warners and
Louis B. Lighton at Fox. I read *A Tree* and saw in it material I knew
something about, the streets of New York and the lives of the
working class. I met Lighton and liked him immediately. I thought he
was most honest and I signed up with him. But I had nothing
whatever to do with the script. I didn't write one word of it and this is
true for the next few films too. The first draft was done by Tess
Slesinger and Frank Davis, whom I have never met. Lighton added to
it and made it better. I think I enlarged *Tree* a bit by encouraging
Lighton to put in a little more of the immigration theme than he
otherwise would have because it meant something to me.

*You took notes during the shooting.*

Nick Ray was some kind of an assistant during the shooting. He
hung around, took notes. He edited them for himself and gave me a
copy. A lot of them were influenced by Lighton and others were my
own thoughts or things I said. Nick liked that kind of generalisation
on aesthetics, etc. He is a dear and sweet man who has had a hard
life.

*In these notes you quote Lighton, about the hero: 'The hero should
not be written better than you or I. You must recognise him as a*

*fellow-human. Then, under special circumstances, he becomes better than you or I.'*

That's pretty good. That's Lighton all over. No wonder I liked it!

*Or: 'At the end, a person should say to the hero: "Gee! You did a great job" and the hero shouldn't know what the hell the other man is talking about.'*

That's marvellous!

*Were there any cuts in the film? James Agee wondered for instance why the tree was absent from the film.*

Not that I remember. I don't think we ever featured the tree as a symbol, though it is a symbol, because it is the only tree that will grow through concrete.

Lighton was very kind and patient. He surrounded me with help in the various areas where I was uncertain, like the camera, where I did not know one lens from another. At the beginning Leon Shamroy seemed sort of harsh; after we shot a couple of days he proposed to Lighton that he should co-direct with me. I refused, but there was some justice in what he said, because I just staged the scene as I would a theatre scene and then he determined where to put the camera and so on. I owe a lot to him. He has a gruff manner but he is a good cameraman. He started in documentary.

*What were the conditions of your contract?*

A film a year, for five years. I did not have cutting rights. I had consultative rights on casting, etc. I didn't have anything special. I didn't get a lot of money either.

*How did you use the setting in that first film?*

This was the beginning of something that was a catastrophe on *Sea of Grass*. I was naïve and I didn't expect the scenery would overwhelm me that way. The scenery in *A Tree* was rather good, but there was something essentially false. If we had shot in New York on the East side, it would have been truer to life. But much worse than the scenery – the rooms were too clean, too nice, too much the work of the property man – were the hairdressing and costumes. They looked like magazine illustrations. The only truly correct thing on the visual side of *A Tree* was the face of the little girl, Peggy Ann

'The only truly correct thing on the visual side ... was the face of the little girl';
Peggy Ann Garner in *A Tree Grows in Brooklyn*

Garner. Because her father was overseas in the war, because her mother had problems, because she herself was going through a lot of pains and uncertainties, Peggy's face was drawn and pale and worried. It looked exactly right. She was not pretty at all, or cute or picturesque, only true. It was also my idea not to have any background music but just source music – the sound of an organ-grinder and so on. But my luck on this film was to have this congenial, affectionate, mutually trusting relationship with Lighton.

*What was your impression of a big studio?*

I was rather overwhelmed by it. But you remember that in my childhood I kept saying: 'Survive, survive.' I have a tough shell; I protect myself and stick to my business, to what I can do. I was able to get the confidence of the actors very quickly and to direct them fairly well. We soon had a good unit with Dorothy McGuire who liked me – and I liked her – with Jimmy Dunn who was uncertain enough and so dependent on me, and the little girl, and Joan Blondell.

51

The big studio did not matter really. It was overwhelming but I just stayed with these five or six people. The rest I left to Leon Shamroy – the grips, the machinery, etc.

Essentially *A Tree* is a tiny story. In the same way as *East of Eden* is the scale of Julie Harris's face, and the little flicker in her eyes, so *A Tree*, too, is an intimate, interior story. The outside has to be there but what is important is that I get the light in that little girl's eyes, the expression on her face, the feeling in her soul. At that time I was separated from my wife, I missed my children, and my own little girl, so I had an extra feeling about a child's love for her father which you find in the film. My wife was puritanical and so was the character played by Dorothy McGuire. But I wouldn't direct this movie at all in the same way now. I haven't got the same vocabulary now – it is a sentimental story and I don't believe in that now. I would never have made Dorothy McGuire as sympathetic as she was. Although she did well, she was miscast: she is an upper middle-class girl. She should have been a working-class Catholic Irish girl, much tougher and more narrow in her values.

*Did you direct actors differently from in the theatre?*

No; I directed actors the same way: I read first, and worked slowly and built each scene very carefully. Actually the movement of the scenes is not bad. What I would do differently is the interpretations of the characters. I have nothing against this picture, but I was not sure of myself, the whole thing was a mystery to me.

*Why did you go to MGM for your second film?*

Because they owned *Sea of Grass* and I wanted to do it. I didn't have an exclusive contract with Fox, I just had to do one picture a year for them. The story of *Sea of Grass* was told me first by Lighton who had worked on it. What attracted me in the subject was the size of it, the classic American story. The cattle are driven off the land by the farmers, the land is broken and made into farms, the pioneers who came there and took the country over are gradually ousted by the farmers, the most bourgeois and safe people. It relates a little bit to *Wild River.* I could still make that story, but to do it right I would have to do it like Flaherty, to go out and spend a year with unknown actors, in the country, where there is grass and cattle, where men's faces are like leather, whereas Tracy's face by that time in his life looked like the inside of a melon, all soft and sweet.

My main interest in *Sea of Grass* really was a feeling, which is shown in *Wild River*, that when history changes, something wonderful is lost. I didn't get a good script either, but that was not the problem. I could have done something with what I had except that I allowed myself to be deceived and I deceived myself. I wanted to prepare that production myself and I went to the office of the producer, Pandro S. Berman, whom I didn't know. The first thing he said to me was: 'I have ten thousand feet of the most wonderful background stuff.' He showed me scenes of rolling grass and I didn't know what it was for – I was naïve. What it was for, of course, was back projection. It became apparent after a few days that none of the picture was going to be shot on location – and it was a picture about grass, country, and sky! Now, if I had been knowledgeable, strong, confident, if I had protected my own dignity, I would have quit. But somehow I was trained not to stop, to find the best solution possible. I don't do that any more. I quit now. The second disaster was the casting. I admired Tracy, I thought he was a wonderful actor. He is dead and I don't want to say anything bad about him, but in effect I found that he did not like horses and horses did not like him. He is supposed to play a man who spends most of his time on a horse. He was rather plump, not a Western type, a little lazy – only able to do things a few times and then losing interest in them – a little inert, not fierce at all, rather Irish and sly, very funny, very convivial, but not at all, in any way, like the type he was being asked to portray. Then the middle-class girl, who was supposed to come out from the East to become his wife, was played by Katharine Hepburn. She is an upper-upper-class girl who wanted then above all to be a big Hollywood star. She is a most intelligent and very decent person, but every time she went to the bathroom to take a piss in that picture, she came out with a different dress. And all the dresses were very nice, but not at all lived in. There was always a rationale for these things: the girl brought her trousseau out West and so on, but the effect of the picture was a lot of pretty illustrations.

In the first few days we did a scene, a sort of farewell scene between Melvyn Douglas and Katharine Hepburn where they had had an affair and they are parting. She cried a lot in that scene and I thought it was wonderful because I had thought she was a cold

Lee J. Cobb and Dana Andrews confront witnesses in *Boomerang*

person – though later I discovered that she cried like that without pretext; if the eggs are cold, she cries. I was very proud of that scene. Pandro S. Berman turned out to be a messenger boy between Louis B. Mayer and myself. He said to me: 'Mr Mayer didn't like the rushes.' I went up to see Mayer and he told me: 'She cries too much.' I said to him: 'But that is the scene, Mr Mayer.' He says: 'But the channel of her tears is wrong.' I said: 'What do you mean?' 'The channel of her tears goes too close to the nostril, it looks like it is coming out of her nose like snot.' I said: 'Jesus, I can't do anything with the channel of her tears!' He said: 'Young man: you have one thing to learn. We are in the business of making beautiful pictures of beautiful people and anybody who does not acknowledge that should not be in this business.'

The whole shooting was a disaster for me personally because I didn't behave right. Furthermore I found out that MGM was not run by Pandro Berman, not even by Louis B. Mayer, but by Cedric Gibbons, who was the head of the production department. He was the one who set the tone for the whole studio: glamour, everything pretty like the cover of the *Saturday Evening Post*. All those fellows wanted three things. One: never offend anybody. Two: make everybody want to go to the movies. Three: organise the movies as a business. And as soon as you organise an art as a business, you're in trouble right there. That's why those old directors got so tough: they had to be, to survive.

Boomerang *is your first contact with reality on the screen.*

Not only that, it was the first film I made in my own way; there were five professional actors – the others were non-actors. It was entirely made in Stamford, Connecticut, thirty miles from my house. We shot day and night in that city. The film was made by an undistinguished cameraman whom I never heard of again. All he did was put the box up and photograph what I told him. I had excellent faces in that picture. I shot the insides of jails and I did everything I thought right and although it's a trifling story, it has an air of reality. I could have done better with a lot of it, especially Dana Andrews who is the only one who looks like an actor to me. There is a dramatic trick in it: it turns out there is a villain, Ed Begley, and at a certain point the author uncovers him: 'There is the bad man.' Actually civic corruption is much more widespread. Not only one villain but a lot of other people would be involved. It is much more complex and I know that now. There is a simplification here of something which is basically true.

*It is a very mixed cast.*

Yes. There are people from Hollywood, people from the Group Theatre, people from the town, Arthur Miller, whose play *All My Sons* I had just produced, and even my uncle Joe Kazan, the hero of *America America*, then an old man. He always complained about the actress he had to play with. He said: 'She doesn't know how to act,' though of course he had never acted in his life himself, and he was always bitching and feeling up the young girl on the set.

But the value of that picture is that it made me feel, this is my medium. I don't think the picture is great, but I wanted to make another picture like it: it led to *Panic in the Streets* and then *On the Waterfront* and *Wild River*. I could go into an environment and make a film with the people around, a few actors maybe, or maybe not. It was the opposite in everything to *Sea of Grass*.

*It was produced by De Rochemont, of the* March of Time *series.*

I liked him, but all he did on this picture was send me the script. I worked very hard with Murphy on the script. I thought: 'Here is a picture on location, and here is a pretty good story and I really will be able to do this picture the way I think pictures should be made.' It was our neo-realism, exactly at the same time as *Paisá*, but of course in no way as good as *Paisá*.

*In your first films, there is a belief in American institutions: the health officer in* Panic in the Streets, *the judge in* Pinky, *the district attorney in* Boomerang.

That's right – the belief that the good in American society will finally win out – which I don't believe any more. I think when we lost faith in the Soviet Union at the end of the thirties, a lot of us said: 'Our basic institutions are good but are corrupted by individual people,' but later we realised that the corruption is general, throughout. It affects the good people, including Roosevelt and Kennedy.

*It was the first time you worked with Darryl Zanuck.*

Yes, but not much. He wrote me notes, that's all. On *Gentleman's Agreement* he worked every day with me: he was a very important man on that picture, he made it against a lot of opposition. I got to know him rather well. At the time of *Boomerang* he was asking me for close-ups. Later he praised my style in *Boomerang* and kept saying: 'Why don't you make pictures like that any more? You used to stage scenes and not take a lot of close-ups. Now you take too many close-ups.' He changed his tune entirely. 'Why don't you let things flow, instead of popping in all the time with close-ups?' He said that on *Zapata*. He regretted that I took so much time when I was so swift on *Boomerang*. And it's true I staged it like theatre scenes with waist shots and full-length shots. Later he held up *Boomerang* to me all the time, but falsely, from the point of view of not spending so much money. Zanuck worked very hard on the script of *Gentleman's Agreement* with Moss Hart. Any day I shot a scene I did not like, I would ask to shoot it again and he would let me. If I didn't like the way a set was painted, which happened twice, he said: 'Paint it again.' He would see the rushes with me and we would discuss them. He was very straight with me. I have no complaints about him except that his basic taste is at all costs to make something that the audience will like. Later I was trying to make films that would disturb, upset the audience. And in the last five or six pictures I did, I tried not to play up to them. I accepted it would not be popular. I wanted it abrasive. I wanted to say: 'Look at your goddamn lives. Terrible things are happening in this country. Look at yourselves. I don't want to kid you any more.' Now Zanuck was hard-working, honest – you always knew what he thought. He never wavered, he never talked behind your back, he was supportive. From that point of view he was great.

*Gentleman's Agreement* was like an illustration for *Cosmopolitan* magazine. Everyone was prettified. It was a series of clichés. But try to put yourself back in American films in 1946 where the word 'Jew' was never mentioned before. For the first time someone said that America is full of anti-semitism, both conscious and unconscious and among the best and most liberal people. That was then a much bolder statement than it is now. In that sense the picture broke some new ground, and Zanuck, Hart and I can take some credit. It was saying to the audience: 'You are an average American and you are anti-semitic. Anti-semitism is in you.' It is better than to say: 'It is a bunch of freaks that are anti-semitic.' And you have to give Zanuck credit for that.

Garfield was the first of the natural off-the-streets rebels, very different from the type played by Cagney or Bogart. He himself was a naïve, pure-hearted, awfully nice boy. He was quite deep in politics, he was deeper in it than a person with his tolerance for pain should have been. I really loved him. I don't want to speak too much about him because it involved people still living and he is one of those cases where you either say a lot or nothing. In fact, I suggested him rather than Richard Conte for the role. Garfield had a natural ebullience, he was life-loving. He would be bouncy, playful . . .

The problem of course was that Garfield was like a regular Wasp, nobody could look nicer than him to the audience, he had no defects, you could not but love him. And in that context, a person like Garfield would have a certain bitterness that would make him not so pretty. And Dorothy McGuire's character was beyond saying! But everything, the photography, the processing, the costumes, the hairdressing, was made to look Hollywood. In *Boomerang* I didn't put make-up on the actors' faces, except on Dana Andrews'. But in *Gentleman's Agreement* the heroine lived in the most expensive house in Manhattan, right over the East River, in front of the Queensborough Bridge, a house that only millionaires can afford. So she is a millionairess because it is glamorous to be rich. At the end, nobody in the audience is left with an unpleasant taste. Somewhere in the middle of it they are shocked a little bit, but I think they were able to get out of it, to say: 'Not me, I am not concerned.'

On *Gentleman's Agreement* I was still in the producer's system. The producer's system was a system where the producer stayed on top and divided the functions. One good thing in Moss Hart's script, though, was the moment when Gregory Peck discovered that he was a little anti-semitic too. But there was not enough of it. It would have been a good story: a man starts to investigate and finds that he is anti-semitic through and through.

*But it was you who suggested that idea to Moss Hart, that Peck should discover some anti-semitism in himself.*

I did say it? My God! Then I was right. You see, I was not strong enough at that time. I should have insisted on ideas like that.

*In your notes you said it is the Jews who make the noise and the fuss because they face the job of breaking down what exists. The Gentiles like it the way it is.*

An interesting thing about *Gentleman's Agreement* is that when Zanuck announced it, there was a terrific uproar from the rich Jews of the Hollywood community. And there was a meeting at Warner Brothers, called, I think, by Harry Warner. At that meeting, as reported to me by Zanuck, all these wealthy Jews said: 'For Chrissake, why make that picture? We are getting along all right. Why raise the whole subject?' And Zanuck, in a polite way, told them to mind their own business. Or perhaps it was Moss Hart who was sent by Zanuck to that meeting as an emissary.

I had thought of Paul Osborn and Lillian Hellman to write *Gentleman's Agreement*. I thought that she, particularly, would have been good for it, would have made it a little more trenchant, painful, a little uglier, harsher than Moss Hart did. She is a very strong woman. But Moss did an excellent, smooth job of dramatisation, the way Zanuck wanted it. I felt about the script that nobody was pushed as in good dramaturgy they should be pushed to a point where they reveal what they are concealing. To me the words 'No Exit' are the essence of dramaturgy. A man is pushed to a wall and against that wall he finally reveals himself. The situation is like a pistol that makes the man finally speak. The one moment in the film I liked best is when Dorothy McGuire describes to Garfield the horror of this anti-semitic party she went to and Garfield says: 'What did you do?', and she answers: 'I was outraged; it felt terrible,' and he keeps saying: 'But what did you do?' I thought that was effective.

*It seems that originally the film was going to be much more like* Boomerang *in its approach.*

That's true: it's what I thought. But it was an expensive production, a Zanuck 'personal' production, with expensive stars and everybody had to look 'good'. I think there is this air of pleasantness in *Gentleman's Agreement* ... It is just a pleasant fucking picture. Everybody has this little problem of anti-semitism that keeps coming up and disturbing their relationship. But in the end Peck and Dorothy McGuire don't go to bed. They are reunited as a pair of lovers but even that is polite. Actually if a thing like that came, their break would be much harsher, much more unpleasant. But Moss was a very nice man, very gentle and kind and genteel.

Pinky *deals with the same kind of subject: somebody who does not seem to be what he really is: here a Negro.*

*Gentleman's Agreement* was such a big hit – and got Academy Awards – that Zanuck naturally said: 'Let's do it again with a Negro.' And this time he got Ford to direct it. Ford started it and shot about ten days. He hated Ethel Waters and Ethel Waters hated him. He did not like the way the picture was turning out. So he went to bed, called Zanuck, and said to him: 'I'm sick. I've got shingles.' Zanuck told me later that Ford didn't have anything wrong, he just didn't want to make the picture. Zanuck called me up in New York and said: 'Do me a favour. Come out, I'll pay you a full salary. Just make the picture for me.' We started from scratch. I worked the best I could but again it is a total dodge. It is not about a black girl but about a charming little white girl. All the unpleasant parts of the subject matter are eliminated. The great scene is where she hugs her black grandmother and all that crap ... Again everybody is very nice-looking, and clean, and neat. It's not a favourite of mine!

Scene after scene that took place in the village where Pinky lived was shot on a sound stage. We had no exteriors, so whatever we could have added to the drama by going down South and really photographing the environment was lost. It was just like a big stage set. By the time I got through with *Pinky*, I was pretty disgusted with what I had done in films. I quit for a while, I took a trip around the country as I did when I was a young boy. I remember one morning in Galveston, Texas, a seaport where they have a lot of shrimp-boats. It was a windy day and I thought: 'My God, look at the life and the colour, the wind and the sea, all the photographic elements, and the smell of it, all the things I don't get in my films!' And I made up my mind that I was not going to do any more films like the ones I had done.

*You know that the film has been criticised for the comments it makes on the Negro question?*

I don't think that the film had any moral, except the general one, of 'how tough it is to be a black'. I never heard a word of resentment from the blacks. It was criticised by some leftist elements. I don't think anybody took the damn film too seriously. It was a pastiche. Taking a subject which has got dynamite in it and castrating it. At that time that sort of liberalism paid off.

*Why didn't you take a black actress for* Pinky?

She was cast already and I had to take it or leave it. And not only was she white in her face but also white in her heart. She was the blandest person I ever worked with. She had no rebellion in her whatever. She is not a bad person, a sweet girl in fact, but she has no inner conflict that I have seen. She must have had things happen to her but she was very controlled about them.

But about that film, you have to accept the fact that it was made before the black movement, etc. It was neither uncourageous nor courageous. It was just Zanuck keeping up with the time and trying to anticipate a little bit what was going to happen. He would take all social issues and turn them into a love story: 'Love solves all, love conquers all' – that was his whole theory. Make a personal story that would carry the social story. It seemed to me it minimised both those films: the sex was unsexual. Generally sex – what goes and does not go on between people – tells a lot about the rest of their relationship in the other problems. But here the sex was not in the story – Jeanne Crain and Lundigan hardly touched. They sort of looked at each other and posed attractively around a tree trunk, which is ridiculous. They must have been hot for each other, something must have happened so that they wavered. But they never wavered! Their attitudes were fixed and mechanical. In other words, the characters served the story rather than vice versa. Both stories were predictable ones. They did not have the quality of life.

*The cameraman, Joe McDonald, was working for you for the first time.*

He was a very easy man to work with. I must say he is a man who made problems that looked serious to me, simple. That was good in one way and bad in another way. I was disappointed in his photography in *Panic in the Streets*: visually, it could have been much stronger. Either he or the lab ironed it out.

*It was during the shooting of* Pinky *that you discovered the importance of the long shot?*

You won't find many notes by me on that film. I didn't work very hard on it. I just got up every day and did the best I could on each scene. But I used to run Ford's pictures all during that time, like *Young Mr Lincoln*. And I noticed that he left the scene with the assassination in a long shot. You heard a little shot of a pistol. And then far away you saw a little smoke go up. And I said to myself: 'If I had that scene to do, I would have a close-up of that man with a pistol, and then a close-up of the other man. I would have gone into it a lot.' And I thought how much more effective it is to let the imagination go. And I began to study these long shots where he tells everything. And I realised that I did that on stage. I said to myself: 'What the hell is the matter with me? I started all wrong in pictures!' Then I made up my mind to make a picture with as many long shots as possible. And it was going to be *Panic in the Streets*. That film was influenced a lot by Ford in the sense that I wanted to graduate from being a director of dialogue to a director of pictures.

*Zanuck was interested in the Negro problem. He wrote to you: 'We give them education but not equal opportunity.' Would you classify him as a liberal at that time?*

Zanuck was always a man of the people. If something was being felt, he felt it. He was a very good geiger-counter. He lay over the society and when things began to move, he noticed them. He was a man of liberal instincts, more than intellect. I don't think he read anything except scripts, simply because he was too busy. He was not a snob. He enjoyed his money and he behaved with some carelessness towards people's opinions. Look at his sex life, for example: he finally did what he felt like; he divorced his wife, which all the other fellows in Hollywood would never have done. They would have continued with their wives and mistresses. He was a decent man. The faults of the pictures I made with him were not his but mine.

*Your personality really appears for the first time in* Panic in the Streets.

I think so too. I had made up my mind not to be bound by the script. It is the first time I threw the script over. We had a property truck with a typewriter on the back of it, on the tailgate. Every morning the writer came to work with me. The script was weak at the beginning but we would redo every scene – that way we were able to use the terrific colour and richness of New Orleans. We shot on the whorehouse streets, in the low bars, in the wharfs. I kept the whole process of picture-making creative instead of rigid devotion to a script. Nobody at the studio checked our work. They did not know where I was going next, we shot all over the city and I had the crew and the cast crazy. Some of them complained I'd suddenly go on a boat or a train. I enjoyed that picture much more than any picture I had made up to then. I picked up people in the street, I teased everybody and kept everything lively. I sort of felt liberated on that picture. It is much better than *Boomerang*. There is more flavour to it.

Widmark was a good friend of mine – I knew him before I did the film, he had played in *Dunnigan's Daughter* which I directed on the stage. Dick is a very real, down-to-earth fellow. It was the first picture in a long time where he was not playing the villain, rolling

Zero Mostel, Jack Palance and Richard Widmark in *Panic in the Streets*

grandmothers down the stairs in wheelchairs with that terrible laugh of his. He played a nice person in *Panic* and he was like that. His relationship with his wife is tart, vinegary, it's a nice relationship, they kid each other in a nice way. Then I put in Barbara Bel Geddes; she still had her big nose in those days. I liked her. Both worked out as a true couple. Some difference between them and the relationship in *Gentleman's Agreement*, isn't it? Mostel was blacklisted; it was the first time he was on the screen again – I got him in spite of the blacklist. Palance had been Brando's understudy in *A Streetcar Named Desire* and it was his first film.

*Did you work with Harmon Jones on the editing?*

He was helpful too, I brought him along, so that he'd have ideas. He was a good cutter. There was a sort of creative co-operative whereas on *Gentleman's Agreement* and *Pinky* Zanuck was on top of it and you were making the scenes that he had carefully worked out with Moss Hart or Phil Dunne.

*In* Panic *as in* On the Waterfront *and other films, you seem to be interested in harbours, stagnant waters.*

What could be more interesting? The ebb and the flow, the come in and the go out, the terrible characters that are around . . . I put a lot of good locations in *Panic*, which helped me for *On the Waterfront*. I could never have made the later film as well as I did pictorially without *Panic*. I learned an awful lot and it was the first time I dominated the cameraman. I said: 'Put the camera here'; up to then I had been in a position where I asked for help from the cameraman and said: 'What do you suggest?' I didn't get arrogant, but domineering. I got my confidence, finally!

*You not only had long shots, but tracking shots.*

Part of that was the fact that sometimes we were in such tight quarters that I only had one place to put the camera and I had to stage the scene so that the emphasis would be the one I wanted. There is a scene inside a boat where there was literally only one place to put the camera.

I didn't feel I was just doing a good job. I enjoyed the fun and the luxury of picture-making. The whole town was ours. Also I kept the actors apart to set them against each other. I don't often do that but sometimes it's helpful for their acting. Palance was sort of insane, and Mostel was a fearless, crazy, terrific guy, and I needled Paul Douglas who played the detective. I also got less psychological. The story is a shallow one about external events, so I was freed from the psychological aspects. The characters were ordinary guys in ordinary spots, coping with outside threats. The Doc was a New Dealer and the policeman a Republican. That was the way we thought, the remnants of my former political training: everybody representing some social political position, but all it amounts to is cliché. Why not have it the other way, it is more interesting: let the guy who is behaving badly think he is a democrat.

For the first time I became aware of the importance of sound. Being in a harbour, you hear fantastic sounds go up and down the river. The river was rising all through the picture and at the end it was coming up over our set, so we had to raise it a few inches every morning. The actors walked on the catwalks that were a little underwater. In other words, the environment was not just something you played against, it was something you played inside of. I also became aware of foreground objects and leaving actors half-hidden, which I used a lot later.

*Did the plague interest you as a symbol?*

I should be able to say yes, but no, I minimised it. It was a device, a way of getting into the various sides of the society and the city.

# 5: Tennessee Williams and the South: *A Streetcar Named Desire* (1950), *Baby Doll* (1956)

A Streetcar Named Desire *is your only experience of making a film from a stage play.*

First, I must say that I had a very great resistance to doing it. It's very hard to become involved in something a second time. I did it for an extremely personal reason, which is that I feel closer to Williams personally than to any other playwright I've worked with. Possibly it's the nature of his talent – it's so vulnerable, so naked – it's more naked than anyone else's. I wanted to protect him, to look after him. Not that he's a weak man – he's an extremely strong man, very strong-minded. But when he asked me repeatedly to make the film of *Streetcar*, I finally said I'd do it.

I thought, 'Well, that's a stage play, I think it's the best play I've ever done. It ranks with O'Neill's best plays, as the best America has ever had. I must try to find visual equivalents for the verbal poetry that it has.' I engaged a screenwriter and we began to 'open it up' from the point of view of time, and from the point of view of where the events occurred, to work backwards into Blanche's past. We had scenes from before the start of the present play, designed to show the circumstances under which Blanche left her home community. We tried to show that she was sort of a refugee in the New Orleans scene. We worked fairly hard for four or five months. Then I read this script and I thought, well, we've done a pretty good job on it. Then I put it away and got involved in doing some other things, casting. I re-read it a week later and I thought it was awful – it had lost the best qualities of Williams' work. Even as story-telling it was bad, because

Marlon Brando, Jessica Tandy and Kim Hunter in the stage production of *A Streetcar Named Desire*

the strength of *Streetcar* is its compression. And I suddenly made a very radical decision – right or wrong, it was radical – I suddenly decided, I'm going to just shoot the play. And I'll even put most of it in the apartment. Most of it happens in Williams' imagination, I'm not going to pretend it takes place actually on the streets of present-day New Orleans. There *is* a streetcar named Daisy Rae – 'desire' – but it has more symbolic reality than actual reality, and I said: I'm not going to *show* her in the streetcar named Desire, that would just be a visual joke, whereas if she talks about it, it comes out fragrant, weighted with her emotions. So I photographed my production of his masterpiece – and I do think it's a masterpiece – almost precisely as he had written it for the stage.

Once I decided on that, I started to work on the *mise en scène* and the décor. I said to Richard Day, who was my art director: 'This community is a very damp community, very hot, like New York was last week – and the walls perspire! I want to see actual water coming out of the walls. I want the walls to be crumbling. I want the walls themselves to be *rotten*, and I want the environment to be a picturisation of decay.' But actually you don't photograph that. In this kind of production where you have people talking all the time, you photograph the people talking. I told him: 'That's a swell job you did, Dick' – but I thought 'Well, a little of it will show, but not very much.' And again I went back to photographing a stage production. Now I don't think I would've done that with any other play I've done; I wouldn't have done it with *Death of a Salesman*, and I liked it a lot. I would have moved that around a lot. But Williams relied on me, he wanted his play done a certain way, he didn't want his words broken into.

The other big decision I had to make was who to put in the film. In those days I didn't have casting or cutting rights – these came later with *On the Waterfront*, because Spiegel was in a bad position. From then on I've always had those rights, but I didn't have them then, so it was a matter of discussion between the producer, a guy named Charlie Feldman, a nice, agreeable but not very strong man, and myself. I urged that we use the original cast, and he would not go for it. Finally, after much hassling, we came to an agreement that we would have one movie star in it. Brando was not a star in those days, his first picture had not come out yet – a picture with Kramer, about paraplegics. Feldman wanted Vivien Leigh, and finally I agreed, with the understanding that I could have all the rest of the cast I had had in New York, which was in the spirit of sticking as much as possible to the original stage production.

*Didn't you make some changes, towards the end?*

I think the end of the stage play is better than the end of the film. It's not, to me, as dramatic as the other. I've always felt, about Williams, that there is a residing ambivalence in everything he does; which means that very often you can look at events and know they can either go one way or the other. They're not like they are in Miller, 'this is *it*'. When you watch Williams' plays, you have the same feeling that you have in life, that you cannot anticipate what will happen next.

What did bother me a lot was a thing I had no control over at that time: the censorship cuts made to satisfy what was then the Breen Office. There was a big controversy about that, and finally it was cut behind my back, after I'd left. It was a small cut, of 40 seconds; but I felt very badly about it, and I still do, because it was a wonderful

*A Streetcar Named Desire*: Marlon Brando, Kim Hunter

scene Kim Hunter had when she was responding to Brando calling her from the bottom of the stairs. They said it was a moment of orgasm, which only shows that the priests who are the censors don't know anything about orgasm, don't know anything about any kind of relationship between the sexes. It was nothing, it was just that she was excited by him, she was excited by his need for her, she heard his voice desiring her, and she responded to it. That's all it was, it was a perfectly natural thing. I think that cut hurt the picture a tiny bit. Backward elements within the organisation of the Catholic Church were determined to keep a certain amount of power for their censoring organisation. And they did make themselves felt in *A Streetcar Named Desire*. There was a particular priest, whose name I've forgotten, who met with us and made several requests for changes. These were disguised; he made a point of saying: 'These are not requests for changes, I'm only telling you what bothers us and what would make us give this picture a C rating if they were not somehow met.' It was quite a clear threat. But I fought very hard on this, because I had very strong grounds, because the play had been acclaimed. The changes were finally made without notifying me. I found out after Warner had agreed to make them. I had no legal ground to stand on, all I could do was write an article in the *New York Times*. And the villain of the article was Jack Warner, who had gone behind my back. I said everything, naming names, just like I do with everything. I named who did what, I named the priests, and I said what I thought of them. The interesting thing is, I thought Jack Warner would be hurt by it, but he was not. I realise you can't hurt these people, you can't insult them, because they can say they don't think less of themselves for it! You say, 'You did a very underhand thing,' and they say, 'Sure, I did. I do underhand things all the time.' And you can see it doesn't hurt at all. Anyway – they won.

The main problem I had with that production was that Vivien Leigh – whom I was very fond of, I still think of her tenderly – had played the part in England, under the direction of her husband, Laurence Olivier. He is a fine theatre artist, but still, what he saw in the play was something an Englishman would see from a distance, and was not what *I* saw in the play. She kept telling me, the first week, 'When Larry and I did it in London –' and I had to keep saying, 'But you aren't doing it with Larry now, you're doing it with me.' It took several weeks to break her down. So, in my opinion, the first two or three reels of the picture are not too good. Then, somewhere around the second or third reel, she and I got together, got an understanding; and she became enthusiastic about what I was saying to her. And we became very close – and I really loved her. I think the last half of *Streetcar* was excellent, and I was really awfully glad she got an Oscar, I think she deserved it.

*The blues piano music was changed into an orchestra.*

I don't think in the theatre we ever had the blues piano the way it's described in the script – I think we had a small jazz ensemble playing blues. Blues is the national emotional music of the blacks in this country, and the effect was a poetic wedding of the feeling of pain and isolation the blacks had in the community, and the way the pseudo-aristocratic whites felt. There was nothing changed about that in the picture and Williams wouldn't have allowed it if he thought it was wrong. He liked the music. It was by Alex North, but the vocabulary of the music was all blues.

*In Williams, contradictions lead to tragedy, whereas in your work they are lively, they lead to dialectic.*

Williams once made a remark to me, that stuck in my mind: 'There should always be an area in a dramatic character that you don't understand. There should always be an area of mystery, in human characters.' In his notes Dostoievsky says of Prince Myshkin: 'The Prince should be everywhere mysterious. He should be unexplained.' Williams too tries not to explain, whereas in my training as an actor we had to justify the way everybody behaved, we had to explain to ourselves the reasons, so we could recreate the experience out of which that behaviour came . . . And then Williams criticised some of my work with other people; he said: 'People don't change as much as you have them change.' I didn't say anything; I thought they did. But I realised there was a difference between the way he and I approached life. I think he is closer to the feeling of death moving in on him. Somebody once said that you couldn't do good work in dramatic form until you had included the possibility of your own death. He lived with this, he lived with death all the time, he was brought up in it.

Let me make a parallel. Blanche Dubois, the woman, *is* Williams. Blanche Dubois comes into a house where someone is going to murder her. The interesting part of it is that Blanche Dubois-Williams is *attracted* to the person who's going to murder her. That's what makes the play deep. I think one of the best things I did for the play was to cast Brando in it – Brando has the vulgarity, the cruelty, the sadism – and at the same time he has something terribly attractive about him. So you can understand a woman *playing* affectionately with an animal that's going to kill her. So she at once wants him to rape her, and knows he will kill her. She protests how vulgar and corrupted he is, but she also finds that vulgarity and corruption attractive. Harold Clurman directed the road version of the play, and he saw the play as almost symbolic, as though Blanche represented Culture that was dying, Culture being devoured by the aggressive, cruel forces around it in American life. He saw Blanche as a heroine. I didn't; I saw Blanche as Williams, an ambivalent figure who is attracted to the harshness and vulgarity around him at the same time that he fears it, because it threatens his life.

Thinking about that helped me clarify for myself my own feeling about the ambiguity in character. I saw this attraction/repulsion, fear/love thing all around me. I see it all the time − I tell you, I see it in marriages, in love-connections between people where there's resentment at the same time as there's love. It isn't only that I'm attracted to it as an artist − it is the *truth* for me, and I think that when you don't have that in a work, the work suffers, not in regard to subtlety only, but suffers in regard to truth-telling. As I began more and more to assert my own view of life, I expressed these contradictory impulses in my films. I found repeated in them a sort of psychological gesture, where someone both embraces another and strikes at him, like James Dean embracing Raymond Massey at the same moment that he throws down the money that he saved for him. Hate turns to love and both are expressed in an action. This is all through my films, even in the comic version. Karl Malden both resents and loves Carroll Baker, Eli Wallach is attracted to her and scorns her at the same time. In *The Arrangement* the husband is resentful of his wife for many reasons but at the same time he feels safe in her hands and in her loyalty and devotion. The greatest act of love that Stavros makes to the girl in *America America* is when he says to her: 'Don't trust me.'

As my films became more my own and, in my opinion, more mature and more expressive of the true human state, they expressed that kind of ambivalence, and also the idea that most bad is done in the name of good. The sexual act has also in it attraction and resentment. For a while sex is pure and romantic, but very soon, there is an element of resentment. Sex, as I see it, is often a cover for many different kinds of psychological traits, brutalisation, bullying, seeking favours. The difficulty in life is not when you love somebody but when both feelings exist at the same time. And this is my relationship with America. I really love it and have great resentment against it. At the bottom there is a great affection for the country; I like it better than any other country I have been in. If I had to choose where I want to live, I would still live right here, in Sandy Hook. And I am attacked from opposite quarters: some people, because of my testimony, say that I am reactionary but many more say that I bite the hand that feeds me, that I am anti-American. There are also constant fires in my pictures. It is a way of expressing what I would like to do with certain aspects of American life. So I play that out in fantasies.

All this is clearly said in the book *The Arrangement* when you have the sense of rebirth in the chapter about the fire. 'Unless we die, we cannot be born again,' the Bible says, and it is one of my deepest feelings. I have had more ups and down than most other people but I always felt that one had to turn against oneself, to turn against one's past. I've often withdrawn and turned against what I did – I believe it is the nature of an artist. Sometimes you have to go underground for a while, to know a personal defeat, to kill yourself. In that sense *The Arrangement* is the most personal of my films. In *America America* Stavros wants to kill his old life, he hopes that he will be washed clean so that he can start again. And the same is true with this country. With Eisenhower we nearly died. Then there was a revolt. What happens with the young people is terrific: nowhere have politics and culture been so linked. And the same happened after the Depression with the New Deal.

In my pictures, I constantly have people in an entirely antagonistic relationship eating a meal together. People in conflict are forced by social convention or family custom to eat together. That's a perfect example of dialectic in Marxism, where there's an element that holds them together and an element that pulls them apart. There's a tension, they're trying to get out, but this thing keeps them together. And that's all through my films. In *Baby Doll* there's a long, bitter scene where they're trapped, together, with this food.

*You and Williams thought about* Baby Doll *early in 1952 and the film wasn't made till 1956.*

Originally we were both thinking of combining four one-act plays, *Twenty-Seven Wagonloads of Cotton, The Unsatisfactory Supper, This Property is Condemned,* and *The Last of My Solid Gold Watches.* I used only the first two. It really started in the Actors' Studio. One of the experimental works I did there was a scene from *Camino Real.* That's the way Williams got introduced to the Studio, he saw that experiment and liked it very much. And when we got to talking about it, I told him there was a good movie in *Twenty-Seven Wagonloads of Cotton,* and he jumped at the idea and said: 'It would be great.' Then I thought to add something from the other three stories, each one making a progress. It would go from one story, then the focus would change to another story, and I was not thinking of it as a unified story, at that time. Then I changed my mind. There was a

73

girl at the Studio, who was just a beginner, named Carroll Baker; she wasn't a member, even, she was just like an apprentice there. Williams' heroine in *Twenty-Seven Wagonloads of Cotton* is a big, fat girl, so I said to him one day: 'There's this girl who has many of the inner qualities of your heroine, but she's not fat – would you like to see her?' So I did an improvisation with Carroll Baker and Karl Malden. The minute Williams saw Carroll Baker, he wanted to put her in the film.

Then I began working on the movie, a little bit here and a little bit there, just to feel it out, and I kept facing the problem of structure, and instead of doing what I first thought, an anthology movie, I decided to make a unified movie. I threw out *This Property is Condemned* and *The Last of My Solid Gold Watches*, but I used *The Unsatisfactory Supper*, that is the old lady and the scene of the supper. Here again, I was working as a writer in disguise, behind the scenes; when I showed the thing to Williams, he liked it. I said: 'You must work on it, though, you're a really great writer, and I'm just a constructionist – or trying to be.' And he said he would but he never did much. He was writing another play at the time, and he would suddenly write a few scenes and send them to me with a note 'insert somewhere'. Some I used and some I didn't; he didn't seem to care. Finally I was desperate, because I had no ending to it. I had got Warner Brothers to finance it, everything was set up, and I said: 'Tennessee, we have no ending!' He said: 'Well, I promise you I'll work on it.' So I said: 'Well, I haven't got much time now, you'll have to come South with us.'

He had a dread of going to the South. He said: 'Those people chased me out of there. I left the South because of their attitude towards me. They don't approve of homosexuals, and I don't want to be insulted. I don't want my feelings hurt.' I said: 'No one is going to hurt your feelings; you're a world-famous, Pulitzer-Prizewinning author, they're going to flatter you! Come on down there, for Chrissake, and help me, and enjoy your fame in your home town.' So he said: 'All right,' and I finally got him to move into the hotel, in Greenville, Mississippi. He swims every day; and he came to me a couple of days later and said: 'I'm leaving.' I said: 'Why?' He said: 'I can't find a swimming pool.' So I said: 'God damn it, I need an ending to this film! You can't use the excuse of a swimming pool to leave, Tennessee. You're leaving me in the lurch! I have a cast, I have a big crew down here; and you're talking about there's no swimming pool!' Then I said: 'I'll get you a swimming pool if I have to build one.' I called the people of the town together and I said: 'We've got to find a swimming pool.' They found a pool, but it was cracked, without water in it. They started to repair it; I went back to the hotel and there was a note from Williams: he'd left town! He'd left me there! The next thing that happened was typical of him – after he's done something bad like that, he does something brilliant. In a couple of days he sent me an ending, which I thought was wonderful. And it's essentially the end that I have in the picture.

I said to him later: 'What the hell did you leave me for, that way?' He said: 'People were passing by in the street and looking at me funny.' So I never saw him again until the picture was done.

*The ending in the book and the ending in the screenplay aren't the same. In the book, they stay together and the husband is going to be punished; but in your film it's much more believable. He probably won't be condemned, and Vaccaro will not come back to the girl.*

He must have revised it. That's funny, I don't know what made Williams change it. At the end of the movie both men leave her. They are fighting there, having trouble out in the dark, and the last thing we see is Carroll Baker asking the old lady: 'What'll we do now?' And the old lady answers: 'I guess we'll wait and see if we're remembered or forgotten,' which I think is a great line. And that's the way it ends: you don't know.

What interested me most was the humorous poetry of it, the humanity of the thing. The film expressed a great deal of affection for the South. They're very hospitable to you. They send you presents, you give them presents, like the Greeks in Europe. But I abominate what their tradition is with the blacks. We had several episodes of protecting blacks from the police there. Once I hid a black man all night in one of our trailers; the police were chasing him, they were going to put him back in jail and we helped him get away. All these whites, they really despise the blacks. But I found them in other ways the most lovable, generous people. They're the closest to Europeans I've seen in this country, in the sense that they are self-entertained, not machine-entertained; they have great affection for each other and for the country life; they are full of hedonism. The USA is supposed to be a pleasure-loving country, but there's no pleasure in the big cities at all. Nobody gets any pleasure except by drinking beer and watching television. But these people were full of pleasure. I used to go on weekends with them, before the picture and during the picture. I used to go to taverns, or on their boats, or fishing and I just loved them. They liked *Baby Doll*. As I remember, they wrote it up well. They didn't say: 'That damn Jew from New York is patronising us.'

What I tried to express was: all right, these events are going on, but essentially something affectionate and dear and human is changing. I tried to like everybody, to find everybody sympathetic and amusing. That was the first time I tried to do that. Also, I tried to cool my loyalties. Up to now I'd always said: I'm for this side, I'm against that side. I'm against the gangsters on the waterfront. I'm for Marlon Brando's character. In *East of Eden* I'm for the bad brother, I'm against the good brother and his father, who's also a puritan. See what I mean? In this one, I tried to deal with an equal balance of relationships. I intended too to make the characters grotesque. It was like an animated cartoon. I think the film is very funny and then every once in a while I feel sad – how ridiculous and sad they are. I tried to mix it up. But mostly my reaction is one of amusement. You laugh at it out of pity. It's tragic. By the way, I tried to get Brando to play Vaccaro but he refused. Vaccaro is a small-time businessman, a hustler. He has no love for the girl. We're not dealing with a love story and not even with a sex story. There's not much sex in it. He takes it all as a stunt, just to see how far he can go. She's not really very aroused sexually yet. She becomes a woman after she's aroused by him at the end, but at the beginning she's a little girl, she wouldn't be a very good lover. She sucks her thumb for the obvious, simple reason that she's still a baby. She's not grown up. That's all, that's all I had in my mind: arrested development. I didn't want to do anything dirty with it at all. To show the act, that's not erotic. But what is erotic is: will he get her or won't he? Will she get him or won't she? And how do they go about it? The awakening of desire is erotic, and so is the presence of desire before it's fulfilled.

*Baby Doll is different from other Williams works which usually involve older women.*

In his plays you also have the young man, the virility that will rejuvenate. In *Baby Doll* there is the dark, fertile outsider who is brought into a dead area and will rejuvenate it, too; he's the new life

*Baby Doll*: Carroll Baker with her husband (Karl Malden); and (*below*) with her lover (Eli Wallach)

coming in. And in the original play she was a big, fat girl who hardly moved and just sat in a chair drinking Coca-Cola. I admired Carroll Baker. During shooting, I got her scared for the need of the role, throwing plaster at her and having the stage-hands move the floor of the attic. She complained to her agent who came to inspect the set, saying it was unsafe, that she'd fall through! But she had great courage: a lot of the film was shot in a drizzle. When she was doing the close-up in the swing, she had an electric blanket, and an electric heater blowing up her dress, to keep her warm! It was January and so damn cold. We had only two or three takes for those shots. I rehearsed it all with the camera, and then I said to her: 'Okay, we're gonna do it. And I want you to come, as near as you can.' Since she was from the Actors' Studio, and new in it, she wanted to show me she could put her whole heart into whatever she did. She'd be as naked and transparent and unguarded as possible. I made her hair straight, and sort of scroungy-looking. A woman who is very beautiful and very unkempt is very attractive to me. She didn't like the idea at first, but after a while she did.

*In* Baby Doll *you are dealing with another conflict, the one between fantasy and reality.*

I like the film *Baby Doll* better than the film *Streetcar* and the reason is, it's more ambivalent. It combines comedy and social significance, passion and farce. I guess you could call it 'black comedy', except that every time you put a label on something, it diminishes it. I think *Baby Doll* has faults; more than *Streetcar*, but it's more attractive to me maybe because of the playful, irreverent, cruel attitude. It's like when you watch an animal that has caught another animal and plays with him before he kills him, or he might even let him go. I think it's an unusual film, and when I see it, I'm delighted with it.

It's visually in a totally different area from *Streetcar*, it's really in the South, and it uses realistic elements in a fantastic way – there are scenes, visualisations, that are both real and completely fantastic. What I like is to find the poetry in very ordinary things around us. One of the things an artist can do is say: 'Here, you just walked by something, you just didn't look at it, turn around and look at it, see now how that is?' I felt that in *Baby Doll*: here's a real, ordinary Southern community, Benoit, Mississippi, where we were for four months. Everything in it is real. Yet it all looks sort of fantastic, doesn't it. And I think it's just that I, as an outsider, was able to see things.

*Streetcar was* rooted in Southern social reality no less than *Baby Doll.*

In fact there are, in *Streetcar*, symbols of social classes, of economic classes, but not of political classes. Blanche is recognisable in this country as a *déclassée*, disoriented, disenfranchised, formerly upper-class Southern girl. It's almost a cartoon now. Stanley is recognisable in this country as a garage mechanic who comes out and swaggers around your car and overcharges you. Stella, as a girl who has run away from her parents – all she wants in life is to be fucked as he's fucking her and to be happy that way. But they're also recognisable as social symbols, as the movement between the classes socially is suggested by the symbols of the characters in that play. Once I decided to make an ambivalence clear, I would say: I'm now going to show Stanley's good side, I'm now going to show his corrupt side. I was attracted to almost insoluble character combinations.

*Schematically, one could say that you combine Miller and Williams, the interest in both social issues and sexual problems.*

Williams, by the way, is political in the sense that he supports any cause that is truly liberal, in every way he can. But it's always pure, it's always immediate, it's not calculated. And it's always personal. I'm not a combination of Miller and Williams. I think I *started* more like Miller and *became* more like Williams. I think at the time, when I did *All My Sons* with Miller, I was very like him, and Miller was very like me. I think Art later tried, in *After the Fall* for example, to see both sides of things. Art is a swell man. He too began to feel that that sort of definiteness, that sort of clarity was not fertile artistically. At least, he says so. I don't find it as much in his work as I wish, but I do see him trying.

*Baby Doll* paved the way for a certain frankness in the expression of sexuality on the screen.

Yes, it did. And it was hurt a little by censorship. Because I meant to keep a certain mystery in the film, it was never made clear what happened. When Silva (Eli Wallach) lies in the crib and she's tucking him in, there's a fade-out. Then he's fast asleep and she's sitting at the foot of the crib. It's utterly unimportant what happened – the exaggerated importance attached to any physical act! – but because so much was made of her thumb in her mouth, there was the assumption by some people that she went down on him during the fade-out; or that some sort of overt physical sexual act had been performed. But it really doesn't matter at all, because that's not what the picture is about, and *I* never thought anything did happen. I just thought of him as first teasing her then falling asleep in the crib and taking a nap, like any Italian might do when he's sleepy; or like an animal would do. She just waits for him to wake.

I felt all through that he was rather scornful of her, and treated her in a way that would give him playful, sadistic pleasure. I think he was more interested actually in business, and in getting revenge on her husband, than in having anything to do with her. After all, the United States is full of girls, and the South is full of girls, and just because she's Carroll Baker and the heroine of the picture doesn't mean he should be interested in her! Also, a European *isn't* that interested – you know, it's not such a crucial problem as Hollywood films make it out to be. But because of the film codes I think I left it more ambivalent than I would have otherwise, I shouldn't have had a hiatus of any kind. Despite that, the Catholic Legion of Decency got together and decided that the picture would get a C rating. And I refused to make changes of any kind. I finally convinced Warner Brothers that the notoriety would help the picture. Furthermore, I had the idea of putting a big sign on Broadway, right over where my office now is, Carroll Baker lying in the crib with her thumb in her mouth! It was such a big sign! *A whole city block!* It was like defying the Legion of Decency, it was a great pleasure to do it.

Cardinal Spellman always went to Korea to spend Christmas with the troops. When he came back, he got up in his church, St Patrick's Cathedral on Fifth Avenue, and he said: 'Here I am, I go and see these boys, they're risking their lives for their country and giving everything they have for the safety of our society, and what do I find when I come back? *Baby Doll!*' That was a fantastic joke around New York, you know, black comedy, this damn fool gets up in church and says: 'What do I find when I come back – *Baby Doll!*' And then – here's the interesting part of it – I for some reason got an idea that he hadn't seen the picture, that he'd just got reports from his various bishops and subordinates. I had a friend who was writing for the *New York Herald Tribune* and I suggested to him that he call up the 'powerhouse' – the nickname for the office of St Patrick's Cathedral – and ask directly if the man had seen the picture. Well, my friend never could get an answer. Then the *New York Post*, which is slightly more to the left, got the idea, and they published an interview with me in which I said that he had not seen the picture. My statement was never challenged. The *New York Post* put it in the headlines: 'Spellman Didn't See *Baby Doll*', 'Spellman vs. *Baby Doll*', or whatever. And then they had an editorial saying it was un-American not to see the picture! And the funniest part of it all was that with all this publicity, with all the front-page pictures of Spellman, and of Carroll Baker and of everybody, and the headlines all about the picture – a tiny little picture, a miniaturist's work! – after all that . . . business was just so-so in New York, and very bad in the rest of the country. The Catholic Church, which is well-organised, had priests in the lobbies of the motion picture theatres taking down the names of their parishioners who came to see *Baby Doll* – which of course kept some of them away, and frightened the hell out of the theatre managers and owners, who refused to book the film. So it was an effective piece of censorship. But it didn't teach me a lesson! Now, when you see the picture, it's so mild that you wonder what in hell all the fuss was about.

*In the various Williams plays that you have directed –* Camino Real *and* Sweet Bird of Youth *and* Cat on a Hot Tin Roof *– did your attitude change towards the material he gave you?*

Well, these plays were all different problems. *Streetcar* had no problem, all you had to do was cast it right, and anybody could have directed it. *Cat on a Hot Tin Roof* – I helped a lot, I think, because I had this idea of speaking out to the audience, as if the actors would admit the audience was there as witnesses to their drama. *Sweet Bird of Youth* was a script with a fault, a serious fault: its interest was split between two characters. The central character in Act I, the old actress, disappears in Act II, and I thought that play needed some sort of directorial 'holding up'. So I had an enormous television screen, and I projected things on it. I did some stunts with that play, because I thought it needed it. I tried to produce *Camino Real* in the style of the Mexican-Indian figures of death, the candy skulls and the little wooden, dancing skeletons; I took a lot from a Mexican artist named Posada who is a sort of primitive and influenced Diego Rivera a lot; and I used some of his works, like his dance of death. Williams approved of all this. I put a lot more music in the play than he had, and he liked that too.

*Would he come to the rehearsals?*

He would come after his morning's work. He would always work, say, from around eight-thirty or nine o'clock till around two; then he would have lunch, and then around three-thirty he would come in and watch for a while. If he saw something funny, he'd laugh very loud. If he didn't like something, he'd say 'NO!' out loud, and I'd say: 'Shut up!' and once I told him: 'Don't come to rehearsals any more. *Never* speak to an actress again.' And he never did again, after that, speak to an actress. He was very generous with his praise when he liked something. He liked stars, and he loved women's voices. He was really an old-fashioned theatre man in one way, despite his modernity. He liked a lilting voice, a Southern voice. Of course, the Southern people still have lively conversation, spend their evenings singing to each other and talking together, and having social intercourse in a nineteenth-century fashion. And Williams is not a tense, closed man, you know, the way you might guess: he's a gregarious, open, socially expressive creature.

# 6: The Political Issues; The HUAC; *Viva Zapata!* (1951), *Man on a Tightrope* (1952)

*The HUAC (House Un-American Activities Committee), with which you collaborated by giving names, was not only anti-Communist, it was also against everything liberal that had been done in America since the New Deal, which you supported. Furthermore it was doing to you and to other people what you criticised your Communist cell for doing before the war: forcing people to do things they did not want to do, controlling their thoughts.*

Well, I don't think there is anything in my life towards which I have more ambivalence, because, obviously, there's something disgusting about giving other people's names. On the other hand, I think that when it's discussed now, it's discussed without relation to the period during which it took place. For one thing, at that time I was convinced that the Soviet empire was monolithic (which proved not to be so). I also felt that their behaviour over Korea was aggressive and essentially imperialistic. I certainly didn't like the people on the Right, and I made that clear in all my statements. On the other hand ... well, as I say, it's ambivalent. Since then, I've had two feelings: one feeling is that what I did was repulsive, and the opposite feeling, when I see what the Soviet Union has done to its writers, and their death camps, and the Nazi pact and the Polish and Czech repression – well, Krushchev says in his book what we all knew at that time was going on. It revived in me the feeling I had at that time, that it was essentially a symbolic act, not a personal act. I also have to admit, and I've never denied, that there was a personal element in it, which is that I was very angry, humiliated, and disturbed – furious, I guess

83

– at the way they booted me out of the Party. In a sense they made it impossible for me to stay in. I knew, because in a small way I was part of the machinery, that orders were coming from above, which we, I, were supposed to hand out below. I despised the men at the top; I had affection for some members of the Party, but the cultural man, I really disliked his ideas and what he meant. There was no doubt that there was a vast organisation which was making fools of all the liberals in Hollywood, and taking their money, that there was a police state among the Left element in Hollywood and Broadway. It was disgusting to me, what many of them did, crawling in front of the Party. Albert Maltz published something in *The New Masses*, I think, that revolted me: he was made to get on his hands and knees and beg forgiveness for things he'd written and things he'd felt. I felt that essentially I had a choice between two evils, but the one thing I could not see was (by not saying anything) to continue to be a part of the secret manoeuvring and behind-the-scenes planning that was the Communist Party as I knew it. I've often, since then, felt on a personal level that it's a shame that I named people, although they were all known, it's not as if I were turning them over to the police; everybody knew who they were, it was obvious and clear. It was a token act to me, and expressed what I thought at the time. Right or wrong, it wasn't anything I made up, I was convinced of it. I had behaved secretly for a long time. Our behaviour in the Group Theatre was conspiratorial and, I thought, disgusting: our cell would discuss what we were going to do, then we would go to Group Theatre meetings or Actors' Equity meetings and pretend we were there with open minds. The whole thing was a way of taking over power. Solzhenitsyn describes the same thing. It was something, in my small sphere, that was symbolic of what was going on in the world. I preferred at that time doing what I did, to just remaining, by my silence, part of the thing. Defecting – that would really, to me, be defecting and lying – saying, 'Oh, I don't know anything about it, I don't know anyone, it doesn't exist, you're foolish to think anything like that goes on,' and all that. I never told a lie, I never told one lie; I've never done anything for money. I've never even directed a play because I thought it would make money. I've always done everything for my own reasons. They may not be reasons anyone else has, or anyone else would agree with, but that's the other person's problem.

*Your next films show that in fact you were nearer to the people on the other side than to the people you co-operated with.*

I always said so — I said so in my statement. 'I'm going to make the same kind of films,' I said, 'but I'll make better films.' Anyway, let me just say this: I was given this story about the escape of a circus, *Man on a Tightrope*, and I ran directly into the block I've always had, which is, I mustn't say anything against the Soviet Union — which was automatic. I thought suddenly that I was an automated person, that I didn't have the courage of the truth and of my convictions. I said: if I really believe this — it was a true circus, it really happened — why do I shrink in fear and terror from saying so? What sort of a person am I? I, by my silence, am part of this conspiracy of lying. I believed that many of the Left who testified or refused to testify didn't tell the truth; they told lies. I told the truth. I think it's important that people should know what goes on in their country, behind the scenes, and in this country, particularly, where decisions are made, presumably, and in some cases actually by people knowing what happens. The whole basis of democracy is: tell the people the truth and they'll make up their minds. And I did.

*Man on a Tightrope* — I didn't think the script was very good. The writer, Robert Sherwood, a brilliant and wonderful man, was exhausted, at the end of his life. But I said to myself, I'll get a real small German circus and go on the spot, and show how it really happened. That way I'll lift the other guilt off me, which was painful to me: I mean, I was really ashamed at being so terrorised, so immured in Stalinism. Many of my friends are still unable to face the truth of that situation. The Stalinists here are so terrorised and so automated that they can no longer take stands. These very, very intelligent and really nice people went right through the whole Czechoslovakian crisis recently and they *still* won't criticise the USSR. I think there are a lot of people here who are still Stalinists. I would fight to the death not to let them control me. I really hate them a lot. What I thought, then, was that there should be a strong, non-communist Left in this country. I don't mean the socialism they have in England, where every Socialist prime minister becomes an earl or a lord right away. Today, in this country, because of the youth, there's a strong non-communist Left. They despise the former Stalinists: they say they're liars and that they're irrelevant.

85

*But don't you think that at that time the danger for America, the threat, came more from McCarthy and the extreme Right, which was also trying to get control of the country?*

I never felt that. Other people all over the world have felt it, and I've been criticised on that ground. I never felt that McCarthy was a big threat. In the first place, the man that put him down was a Republican, Eisenhower – a very reactionary, very traditional Republican. The judge that exposed him was also that way. I always had faith in America's process of putting light on her problems. What killed McCarthy was one moment on television, when the whole world saw him whisper to a lawyer sitting next to him – and in that instant they recognised he was a bad man. He *was* a bad man. He was an embarrassment to me and to many of the people on the same side I was on. What I say now to my critics is: look at the work I've done since.

At that time, people wrote articles, they humiliated me in the press. Okay; they were right to fight back for their lives and for what they believed in. But what they said was that I was finished, corrupt and would never do anything again. As is obvious – I don't have to point it out – I began to make good films, really progressive and really deep only *after* that period. The first film I made after that was *Zapata*, which I prepared before, and made during and after. Then *On the Waterfront*. Because of what I'd done, they said *On the Waterfront* was fascist in its ending. Well, it was *not* fascist; it was an exact description of what happened. I felt the workers would be in the same situation again, they had not conquered the corruption. The last thing Lee J. Cobb says is: 'I'll be back.' And he did come back. I knew the waterfront in Hoboken intimately. I spent months there. Schulberg spent a year there. There was an election, after the film was made, in which the 'good' side, our side, lost by something like a hundred votes, out of two thousand – a very small margin. The waterfront has never got any better, it's the same now, just the same.

I have never, because of my nature, felt apologetic about anything I did. I don't say that human beings don't make mistakes; I have often. I don't say that what I did was entirely a good thing. What's called 'a difficult decision' is a difficult decision because either way you go, there are penalties, right? What makes some things difficult in life is: if you're marrying one woman you're not marrying another woman, if you go one course you're not going another course. But I would rather do what I did than crawl in front of a ritualistic Left and lie the way those other comrades did, and betray my own soul. I didn't betray it, I made a difficult decision. It was – it still is. I've never been at ease about it. I've never said: 'Sure, that was good!' It's not that simple.

*You could have made your statement two years before or two years later; but it came at a time when the witch-hunters were trying to control the thought of the American people in a totalitarian way, because it was not only Stalinist communism that they were fighting but any kind of socialism, any kind of intellectual freedom . . .*

But I never felt, because of the job I had done, was doing, and planned to do, that I had been silenced in any way. Rather, I have spoken more freely and more boldly since then. I never said I liked McCarthy, I despised him, I really and truly did, I said that publicly all the time. I said: 'I'm embarrassed at being connected at all with these people.'

*In 1953 you wrote in your notes: 'We must protect ourselves from the Communists, but also from the consequences of our rage at them.' You sensed the possible danger of being on the side of the conservatives by sheer anti-Stalinism.*

All I can say – I don't say it loud, I can't beg anybody's pardon – when people criticise me, is: look at my pictures. I think I've done social and critical pictures ever since. In *America America*, in *Splendor in the Grass*, in *Wild River*, I think I've made pictures that are *Left*. And *The Arrangement* – the book, too. And I'm still called a communist; my name is still on that list. I'm still attacked as a communist; these people on the Right look at my work and say: 'Well, he's still doing the same stuff.' Wait till they read *The Assassins*. I'm going to change my phone number, because I know I'm going to get all kinds of attacks. I don't want to be terrorised. That's why, now, the Left is suddenly beginning to get favourable to me, saying I did a bad thing but looking at my films. In the last two years they've begun to change and to respect me again.

*Do you think that the resentment at what you'd done, at least partly, gave you strength to go on?*

I think it made a man of me. Up to then, I was the blue-eyed boy, everybody's darling; I was both very successful and very Left; I was the living demonstration of how you could be on the Left and still be in the gossip columns and be envied for the money you made. I was essentially an other-directed man, I was really working for the praise of others, for the notices in the papers. This thing made me say: well, not everybody likes me, I've lost many of my best friends (they would pass me in the street and not say anything, not even nod to me). I said, okay, I'm going to satisfy myself now, not the critics, not even my friends. The ironic thing was that I also became vulnerable in the eyes of the movie executives. The first thing they did was to cut my salary down. They said: 'You're damaged goods now, we're not going to pay you that much.' Zanuck or Skouras or somebody actually said to my agent: 'He can take it or leave it, that's all we are going to pay him.' It was less than half what I got before.

*You said* Zapata *was prepared before the HUAC testimony.*

Yes, various things started *Zapata*, but it was my idea. I went to John Steinbeck and I said that I'd been thinking about this man. And John suddenly took hold of it, very strongly. He said: 'I know about him, I've often thought about him,' and he told me he'd be interested in it. But there was something deeper, which was maybe only partly conscious on our part, and that deeper thing was that we were both reaching for some way to express our feelings of being Left and progressive, but at the same time anti-Stalinist. We lived near each other then, were very close friends.

I think that somewhere in the back of my head I'd always been looking for a subject like the great Soviet films that I liked in the thirties – *Potemkin* and *Aerograd*. I'd had the idea of making a film on Zapata since 1935 when I took a trip to Mexico and heard about him. We were interested in his tragic dilemma: after you get power, after you make a revolution, what do you do with the power and what kind of a structure do you build? John thought that he should do research before we even talked any more about it. He was at a loose end: his second marriage had busted up, and he hadn't yet met the girl he was married to till his death – Elaine. So he went off to Mexico and stayed there a while – a couple of months, I think – got Mexicans to help him with the research, and he did a lot of reading himself as he knew Spanish well.

In some subtle way that I only partly understood, *Zapata* was the first film I made which was autobiographical. I was, during that time, really at the peak of my career position, whatever the hell that means — I was more in demand than any other stage director, and I was also the 'two-coast' sort of 'genius' who was working successfully both places. But I was just beginning to question myself as to what I really wanted to do; I certainly didn't want to continue in the rat-race of trying each year to have another success to stay on top; and I was beginning to wonder — questions which came up again a decade later — what were my own feelings about these things, about all issues, about life itself, and my own life in particular. So that the seed of what was to be a lowering of my own position — what people around New York called my 'confusion' or uncertainty — my self-questioning was beginning. In that sense, the figure of Zapata was particularly attractive to me, because after he got all the power that comes with triumph, he didn't know what to do with it or where to put it or where to exert it. He felt about things as I was beginning to feel about my own situation. So all these three things — the fact that he was externally colourful and interesting, the fact that he represented a Left position that was anti-authoritarian, and the fact that in some way he was related to my life story, at that point in my life — were reasons why I became so interested in the subject.

He had also an ambivalent relationship to women. He wanted both a peasant woman and a woman of a higher social level, with more education and greater refinement. What he did was to go outside his class. He moved up into the middle-class, and he had to court her in the old-fashioned ways; he got dressed as a middle-class landowner. And in a way it was his first betrayal of himself, to court a woman that way and to marry that type of person. Later in his life, when she disappears temporarily, he's seen fleetingly with peasant women, following him or looking after him; but this was a move in a direction opposite to the one he stood for publicly. That's the way I looked at it, that's what I had in mind. That's partly why we cast Jean Peters, because I wanted someone brought up as an élite person in a small town.

Anyway, John worked terribly hard and, I think, very conscientiously — he got Mexicans to go into the back-country and find Zapata's remaining relatives, or people who'd known him, seen him. He wrote all the research out in a form which whatever actor played Zapata could understand. I think with any hero who's dead five minutes, different people viewing his career would have different thoughts about him, pointing to different significances. Well, it was the same here, except that there was one subtle difference. I felt that the communists of Mexico were beginning to think of Zapata as useful, a figure they could glamorise in anti-gringo, pro-Mexican nationalist struggles. They thought, especially since he was dead and it was long ago, he could become a useful idol or god to call on. They didn't like our film because it showed him as being unclear. Obviously he was unclear, because he hesitated, and didn't know what he was doing; he was trying to find a new path for himself.

I wanted to make this in Mexico very much, and I submitted the picture to the head of the syndicate of film technicians – a cameraman named Gaby Figueroa. I wasn't very keen on having him photograph the picture; he made all women look like madonnas, and he loved very corny effects like large crowds carrying candles. But when we first met I found him intelligent and agreeable, and we had some good conversations. Then he read the script and his whole face changed. He demanded certain changes; he said he couldn't work on the picture unless certain things were different. Furthermore, he would oppose its being made in Mexico unless we made those changes, and we told him to go to hell. The conversations ended abruptly and we said we were going to shoot it somewhere else. He said an amusing thing: 'Suppose a Mexican company came up to Illinois to make a picture about Abraham Lincoln's life with a Mexican actor playing the lead, what would you think of that?' And I said to him: 'I think it would be great, I'd love to see that.' We left Mexico the next morning. I decided to make the picture in Texas, as close to Mexico as I could, on the Mexican border.

*Obviously* Zapata *avoids both the very faithful biography of the man, step by step, and also the political story of the country. You chose to make sketches, to show various aspects . . .*

When John came back with his research, it was overwhelming; even if it had been shorter, we would still have had to decide on the form of the picture – which story to tell. You could tell a hundred different stories with that material. The story we wanted to tell was of a man who organised himself and his comrades, the people around him in his province, because of cruel and terrible injustices; he organised them to revolt, and the revolt spread because of the repression that it faced, and because its causes were just. And the revolt resulted in a successful revolution. That's the first act.

90

Joseph Wiseman, Brando and Margo in *Viva Zapata!*

We then told the second act, which was that once he got power, he didn't know how he wanted to exercise it. He was bewildered; and he began to find that power not only corrupted those around him, like his brother, but he had also begun to be corrupted by it himself. The third act was that he walked away from it, he walked away from the seat of power and so made himself vulnerable. He lost the soldiers who were protecting him, and the prestige that protected him; he became an easy target for destruction. So we organised John's material around these three movements. Once we did that, we knew what part of the material we wanted to use, where it would fit in and how it would work. I also found a technique of jumping from crag to crag of the story, of preparing an incident carefully but not playing it out in length. I think it was the first film I made that was structurally cinematic, where just a suggestion of an incident tells you more than the full playing out of it; the first picture I did that just jumps like that, where it's a lot of short incidents, held together by a frame that is essentially cinematic.

91

Then the other thing was to find an external style for this, and I found a book down in Mexico, *Historia Gráfica de la Revolución* – from 1900 to 1940 – Archiva Casa Sola. It contained the most complete record of a war I'd ever seen, the detailed story in photographs. The men who had taken the pictures were excellent photographers, and knew how to capture what Cartier-Bresson calls 'the decisive moment', the exact moment when something is at its most significant. Some of those photographs are archetypal. They had a great quality of underplaying horror, that is, there'd be horrors and drama and death there, but it was taken as a matter of course. It was the nature of a revolution to show that and to deal with it. These photographs were of great use to me, and I went so far as to imitate them, in some cases exactly. There's one scene in particular where Pancho Villa and Zapata meet in Mexico City, when they come into a room to be photographed, surrounded by their subordinates and henchmen. I reproduced that scene exactly. I got extras to be made up exactly like the ones in the picture, and I placed everybody in exactly the same position. I rehearsed it many times with the pictures in hand; just as a stunt, I tried to re-create that moment in history so it would be authentic.

I also did something that I was going to do later on other pictures: I went into a small Mexican town named Roma where I was meaning to shoot the picture, and presented myself to the people and to what authorities they had. It was a very sleepy, debilitated town, not prospering at all. Anyway, we said we were going to stay there, and of course they were delighted to have us, because we brought employment with us. I said I would like to make a band of whoever played music, especially people who had been in Mexico twenty, thirty, forty years ago – all the old-time musicians. They all came around with their marvellous old instruments. I chose about a dozen of them and without much rehearsal I had them play for me in unison, not in parts but in unison, the old songs of the revolution and the old, classic songs of Mexico that they remembered. In this way I got the basis of the score. The only mistake I made was that I should have somehow used them to make the actual score. But I gave the tape to Alex North who used it very well, I think. I found that it's a good way to work, because it's using the background to provide the music for you, and it's as authentic as the scenery. We got some terrific musical effects just by doing that. I was thinking at one time

Zapata fights with his brother Eufemio (Anthony Quinn)

of having a 'corrida' — a kind of running song-commentary. It's something that appealed to John and we worked on that, but though the idea sounds good, when you use it repeatedly you can't find a way to make it progress. It started out effectively, but then it got slower, and heavier, and then interrupted the narrative. I never was able to solve it, and finally let it go.

*There's a danger in this type of film that says that every revolution at one moment becomes perverted: it can be seen either as revolutionary, 'Trotskyist', saying that the revolution is permanent, or as very reactionary, i.e. every change brings a new kind of oppression, then why try to change anything?*

We were very conscious that it could be taken to be saying that the revolution was futile. But we tried very definitely to avoid that by saying, at the end, 'The people still think of him, he's still alive,' that at the end he was trying to create the revolution again, that he did

educate himself to a point – in other words, we tried to say that there
*is* a next step, that he was beginning to find it, and that he didn't. We
had that in mind, anyway. And at the end the ritualistic Leftist
becomes a murderer and kills Zapata.

*The* Daily Worker, *a Communist paper, did not attack the film as
being Rightist, but as being Trotskyist!*

My true feeling personally is that in one guise or another, all
revolution is permanent and always will be permanent. I think there
always has to be some struggle within a society to keep it moving
forward, and attack the tendency in people to become crooked, to
become bastards. One of the very effective moments in the picture is
when he discovers his brother is corrupt; but an even more effective
moment is when he discovers that he has become just like the man
that circled his name at the beginning, that *he* did the same goddamn
thing. When the peasants come to see him, he does exactly the same
that the man did to him, at the beginning. So, there you are! The fact
that it troubles him, that he has a conscience about it, seems to me to
mean that he's not that kind of person – that at bottom he realises the
danger and seeks a way to overcome it.

At the time *Viva Zapata!* was made, the communists in this
country condemned it because, they said, I'd taken a revolutionary
hero and made a wavering intellectual of him. All right. Time passed.
Twenty years later the New Left, which is the students, the non-
communist Left, the Left I've always felt an allegiance towards, and
especially an organisation like the Young Lords (the Puerto Rican
revolutionary group I became acquainted with when I was working
on Budd Schulberg's Puerto Rican picture) loved *Viva Zapata!*. They
used to ask me for a print and look at it again and again, just like they
did *Battle of Algiers*, because both made them understand what their
problem was going to be. The scenes of the revolution and of the
unity of the people around Zapata, how the people gathered around a
cause, was something they felt was going on with *them*. It became a
film they showed like an educational picture, on the technique and
the nature of a revolution. The change in what the Left *is* reversed the
attitude towards the picture.

*Wasn't* Zapata *also a revenge for the fact that you couldn't do* Sea of
Grass *as you wanted to, and were making an epic?*

Absolutely right, but I knew a lot more about *Sea of Grass* than shows in that picture. But since, I learned that I had to exert my power and be very tough. I just went my own way. I had a wonderful wife, who, during the shooting, used to get telegrams in the morning from Zanuck, scolding me and saying 'Why are you going so slow?' and 'You're costing me a fortune.' She never showed them to me but she would keep them, and at the end of the picture she gave me about ten telegrams!

*What's missing is any reference to American land seizure.*

Zapata was in an isolated province, though. Where American imperialism was felt very strongly was in Pancho Villa's struggle; he was close to the US border. It was also felt very strongly on the east coast, where there was oil. But much less in Zapata's land, which was arid and stony and had no assets that anybody wanted. Zapata's struggle had a certain purity, because it was based in poverty. When he got to Mexico City, we might have shown American influence there. But he didn't stay there long, he left very abruptly.

*Howard Hawks said that out of a disgusting bandit you made a Santa Claus; and Samuel Fuller said that out of an idealist you made a murderer!*

Jesus Christ! Well, Fuller is some authority on idealism, and Hawks is an authority on bandits! There's one scene in *Zapata* that I didn't like, though: the wedding-night scene. They look too glamorous, they look like Hollywood stars. I also didn't like the way he said 'I can't read' and all that. It didn't seem 'native' to me, it didn't seem out of that book of photographs, Brando looked too gorgeous, I should have covered his top, his body looked too well fed, too classically healthy, too athletic in an American way; he didn't look *stringy*, like a Mexican horse, he looked like a fine American thoroughbred. And *she* looked like an American beauty queen, sort of all made up.

*Do you think there was something 'Russian' about* Zapata *in the sense that you had the sweep, the movement of the people?*

Yes, there was, in that sense. There was even a mystique about the people, in that they were aware, they responded, they were looking for leaders, looking for leadership; they were a force that had to be dealt with. One of my favourite scenes is of the women making

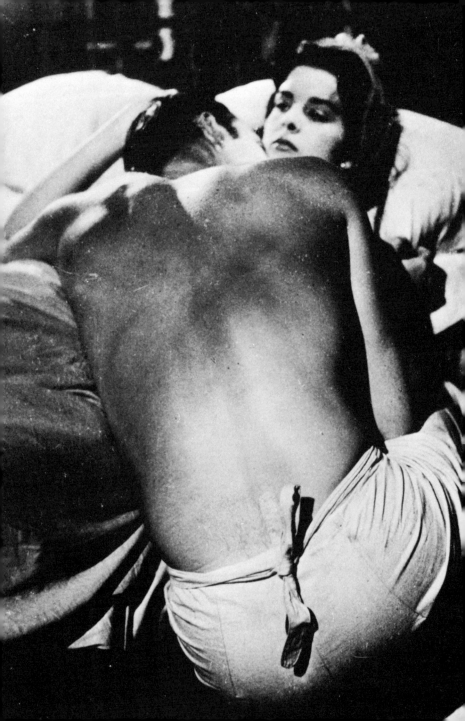

tortillas and hitting the stones, and also the scene when they bring the body back and throw him on the well-top, on the brick platform; and the women are in the shadows and they don't move. I like the way I had the women in the corners, out of the sun, watching the action – sort of like the way I use blacks later in other pictures, you know: watching it, judging it.

*Zapata is the first film where you do not have a professional screenwriter.*

Right. I began to go to authors like Steinbeck, Budd Schulberg, Inge – who were not screenwriters – and I'd say to them, 'Let's do a picture about this.' What I needed most was not the technique of how to construct a screenplay, I needed that help too, but what I needed most was someone who saw in Zapata what I saw in Zapata, or someone who saw in *On the Waterfront* what I saw in *On the Waterfront.*

Steinbeck always loved the Mexican people, he was brought up very close to them. He had written *The Pearl* and made many trips to Mexico before *Zapata.* And after all, what greater authority on puritanism could I get than William Inge? I mean, he's a victim of puritanism, he knows it like someone whom it has hurt.

*With Zanuck you now had a different relationship from the one you'd had on the previous films?*

Yes. In the first place, I still don't know why he did *Zapata.* I guess because I'd made money for the company and he was looking for something exciting and unusual; maybe he liked some things about it, I don't know. It seemed very foreign to him, at that time. I don't think *Grapes of Wrath* was; *Grapes of Wrath* was about people he knew. But *Zapata* just bewildered him. His contribution to *Zapata*, the one I remember most, was the white horse. That was his idea. I don't know where he got it, from an old Western I suppose. And at the time I regretted agreeing to it, though I don't regret it now. I think the white horse works beautifully at the end, where they bring Zapata his old horse as a present. Then, when Brando says to the horse, 'You got old,' I think it's a beautiful moment in the picture. But, as always with Zanuck, he was absolutely straight with us; anything we needed, we got.

The thing he opposed most was Marlon Brando. Brando had not

Zapata with the woman he marries, Josefa (Jean Peters)

made *On the Waterfront* yet, remember. He'd made *A Streetcar Named Desire*, where everybody laughed at his mumbling. He was sort of a joke, an industry joke, because of his terrible speech. I did a test with him and Julie Harris, because I wanted Julie Harris, at first, to play the part Jean Peters played; Zanuck saw the test, and he wired me to say how worried he was. He said: 'I don't understand a goddamn thing the sonofabitch says. Can't you stop him from mumbling?' He said: 'He's too young for it.' He wanted to get – I dunno, some sort of Mexican type. He said: 'This is just an Illinois boy, what the hell are you trying to make a Mexican out of him for?' Well, I couldn't explain it, but after a while he just accepted it and half gave up, and sort of trusted me that it would turn out all right. When the picture was finished, he rather liked it; he wasn't nuts about it, but he rather liked it. But when it started to do no business, he turned against it, and so did Fox. They did very little to promote it, they tried to forget it.

I can understand its lack of success. You're telling the story of a failure. Furthermore, you're telling the story of the expropriation of land by a Mexican failure. There's no love interest that ends the way they want. It goes against so many of the audience's desire to be deluded. I didn't realise it when I was making it. When I saw it afterwards, I thought, how can they like it? But in Turkey or Greece, where they have that problem of land they scream their approval, they yell at the picture!

*It was your second film with McDonald as a cameraman.*

I was more satisfied with his work here and he was a great help to me. He was rugged, in the first place, he would go anywhere and do anything. He likes to work in heat. He didn't do anything to spoil the sand, the dirt, and the desert, the cactus plants; it all came over very well, and I think he did an excellent job.

For the locations, I went down there to look for them long before. I always do that very carefully, because I think it is a critical choice that you make; it can be a disaster, or it can make the picture. I rode all along the US–Mexican border, along the back roads until we came on this town that was originally a Mexican town. It still looked like one. We built a few more little things, just to make a complete square, and that was it. The interiors were real interiors, not sets. We came back and shot a very minor portion on the Fox ranch, near Malibu.

*Had you seen Eisenstein's* Que Viva Mexico?

Yes, but it didn't have much influence on me. It was a very formal, sort of stationary, passive, set style. I read the script, but I didn't get much out of it. It was a poem, really. I don't think it was a good poem, in words.

*Viva Zapata* was a terrific experience for me. It changed a lot in my life and films. When I got through I felt I had a much broader scope ... I was influenced by Eisenstein and Dovzhenko, but now it was a digested influence, I never thought about them while shooting. I used the long shots that I had discovered in Ford, but creatively, whereas I had used them mechanically in *Panic in the Streets*. Because with *Zapata* it was a subject matter I liked.

Man on a Tightrope *was, I think, the only film you made that was about a country you don't really know. Otherwise there is always a kind of physical experience of the places you speak about.*

I tried to correct that by going there; I lived very close to the circus, I lived in a trailer, I played with them. I like circus people. I don't think it's a successful picture. The one part I think is good is the way I showed the circus, and the people in it. What interested me in it is that it's truly democratic and cosmopolitan – there's no race, religion, creed – people are judged by their ability to do a job. I saw there in a microcosm a society that had its own dignity within the world chaos.

What I thought was poor was the love story, and the discussions between the Commissar and the honest man were schematic. I had no chance to change them. Sherwood, the scriptwriter, said to Zanuck: 'I don't want anything changed,' and left. Sherwood had prestige and power, and he had his rights. I did my best with that. Many scenes were embarrassing. They were just statements of politics, rather flat New Deal statements which, by 1952, eight years after Roosevelt, and in the context of a little circus, seemed absurd. I do believe that if I had had a young writer and worked three months more on it, I could have made a helluva good picture. It could have been exciting, colourful, touching, sad, every goddamn thing a picture should be.

*Didn't Zanuck cut twenty minutes of* Man on a Tightrope?

That's what finished me with Hollywood, really. I came back from five months in Germany – I hadn't seen my wife and children, I

hadn't been home – so when I got to New York I called Zanuck up and said: 'Look, while the editor is finishing the first cut of this thing, I'd like to spend a few weeks in New York with my family, and then I'll come out and work with the cutter.' We had been working in Germany on it, so the cutter and I understood each other. In California I had had a nice office in a big building – I was a big shot when I had left. I didn't feel the picture was going to be too good, but I thought that if we worked on it we could make it good. I went to the doorman on my first morning back at the studio and said, 'Where's my office now?' and he said, 'It's down in the Old Writers' Building.' The Old Writers' Building was a building where they put the beginning writers and so on. I got the idea. I said, the picture's a flop in their eyes, or they would have given me my old office . . . I went down to the office, and on the desk was a letter from Zanuck saying: 'I have cut twenty minutes out of this picture. I think you'll like it. Anyway, keep your mind open till we see it together.' I saw it with him and I said: 'I don't like it at all, I'd like the footage back.' He said: 'No, it's terrible, what I cut, it's better this way.' I don't claim that if those twenty minutes had been in, it would have been much better, but I do think that I should have cut it with the cutter first, before showing it to him . . . I made a mistake in putting it in his hands. He's a man who prides himself on his cutting ability. That may be good in melodrama; in the pictures he's done he may have done wonderful cutting, but I don't think this picture was well put together.

I said to myself: 'Well, I'm never going to do that again. Even if I don't make pictures, I'm going to insist on cutting rights.' I had cutting rights for *On the Waterfront*. After it was a big success, I was a producer on *East of Eden*. I had absolute rights on all my pictures.

Cernik (Fredric March) with his wife Zama (Gloria Grahame) in *Man on a Tightrope*

# 7: Working with Schulberg: *On the Waterfront* (1954), *A Face in the Crowd* (1957)

*Much before* On the Waterfront *you were thinking of doing a film about the docks.*

Yes, that was in 1951, before *Zapata*. I spoke to Arthur Miller. There was a struggle within the Longshoremen's Union at that time, and Art knew a lot about longshoremen. He worked in the Brooklyn Navy Yard as a steam-fitter, a plumber's assistant or something of that kind during the war, before he could make his living as a playwright. He knew the waterfront, and I think the idea of a film was his. I was very enthusiastic about it. He began to work on a script; it was called *The Hook*. I don't remember much about the script, but we got quite a way into that thing; the script was completed, and we arranged the financing from Columbia Pictures. Then I got a phone call from Art saying that he had decided he didn't want to do it. I still don't know why he did that. Anyway he called it off, and I was annoyed with him, because I'd spent a lot of time on it. It was an extremely abrupt and embarrassing decision.

*From what you remember, was it very different in point of view from what was going to be* On the Waterfront? *Was it also an individual story?*

No, it was much less an individual story. I have the script somewhere but I haven't read it since. It was very different in feeling. I think Art saw the Un-American Activities Committee coming and there was something that had suddenly developed in his personal life that made him not want to have that film done. Things were much touchier then, people were threatened and on trial and being forced to take stands.

The Hook is a section of the waterfront, 'Red Hook', it's called, but it's also the longshoreman's hook which you hold with the handle, like the communist sickle. You hook the baggage with it. It's seen in *On the Waterfront* – all longshoremen use it. That script was never in good shape; I don't think it was ever really ready to do. What we did with *On the Waterfront* was rewrite and rewrite it. Finally with Spiegel's help and persistence and Budd's hard work, we got a very good script out of it.

On the Waterfront *was the first film you made in New York.*

All the next pictures were made from New York. *Face in the Crowd* was made in a New York studio and on location in Arkansas; *Baby Doll* was made in a New York studio, from a New York office, and on location in Mississippi. I was determined, after my last experience at Fox, to make pictures in the East. I put together the first good crew in New York – Sidney Lumet used it later. Before, they were doing only TV shows in New York.

Part of this decision – a considerable part – was due to my revulsion at the Hollywood environment. This is simple-minded but ... There you go from your house to the studio in a car and you see nothing. In the studio you're in a non-environment, in your house you're in a swimming pool. You never talk to anybody except the crew and your agent, and your friends, who are like you. None of the buildings have any identity, they're all imitations of other buildings. It's all like living in Disneyland. Even the people's tans seem false. I love the West, I love the northern half of California, from Santa Barbara up – I think it's one of the most beautiful states in the Union. But from Los Angeles down to San Diego, that belt there, it's what I like least in American life. It's also very reactionary, hateful, dangerous. That's where Nixon comes from; that's where he chose to live. For good reasons.

But in New York City, if I walk from my house, on that street, down to my office, I see twenty things every day that remind me of the fate of the world, of the nature of the conflicts in the city, of the problems of ecology – everything is all around me, and it's stimulating to me. I can grow in it. I'm in touch with it, things strike me and pinch me and turn me and affect me. In Hollywood nothing happens. I didn't want to be like the others there, more and more attenuated, more and more abstracted, less and less 'in things'.

Priest and longshoremen: Karl Malden in *On the Waterfront*

*On the Waterfront* is a good example of this contact with reality because it is about living issues. And furthermore, it's about an issue that was being decided as we made the picture. Watching me shooting there used to be all the gangsters that we described in the picture! And they'd come up – once a guy grabbed me and was going to beat me up. A longshoreman beat *him* up. I always had a bodyguard a few feet behind me, a former detective on the Hoboken force, he was always close to me. I worked in among activities on the dock. They were loading ships while I was directing. It was my ideal of how I'd like to make pictures.

*There is a difference between the film and the book that Schulberg published after the release. In the book, Terry is killed at the end and the priest has been moved from his parish: it is much more pessimistic.*

Schulberg was responding, when he wrote the book, many months later, to some criticism that was made of the ending. However, the priest was exiled, after we had finished the film. Budd knew that;

104

Budd stayed close to that priest. So he wrote that in. I didn't read Budd's book. But 'Terry' was never found dead; he was still working, I believe.

What we intended to show at the end was that the workers there had found, or thought they'd found, a new potential leader. He had almost been killed, remember? And very often, in the labour movement, a new movement starts with the death of a person, through the memory of a martyr. The boss in the doorway, to me, seems rather futile, when he shouts. The workers gather around Terry, as if they were going to continue their struggle. But after all they have to work for a living, they're not going into some intellectual state of withdrawal from it. It was as close as I could get to what actually happened on the waterfront.

*There's no background to the gangsters' action – we only see a man's back.*

Budd and I wished we had been able to go deeper into the social structure which supports the gangsters. On the other hand, if we had gone more into that, we would have lost some of the unity of the film. It was a tough problem. We would have been diffuse, at that point. I think we probably could have done it with one other glimpse, one other piece of action, if we'd found it.

*The film related, in a sense, to the gangster films that could be said to sum up real American life on the screen.*

That's absolutely true. The first breakthrough into working-class life came through gangster films. They were the first view from underneath.

Face in the Crowd *and* Waterfront *had a journalistic impact.*

Budd has worked a lot as a journalist, but he also works when he writes a script, by immersing himself in the environment, doing research and taking notes. I work more in terms of dramatic symbols than Budd does. The love scenes are the best thing in the film. The scene on the pigeon's coop with Eva Marie Saint is beautiful, and the scene at the bar table with her, where Terry says: 'Don't say that.' Eva is wonderful in those scenes and so is Marlon.

Brando was as close to a genius as I've ever met among actors. He was on a level apart. There was something miraculous about him, in

Terry (Marlon Brando) and Edie (Eva Marie Saint) talk for the first time since childhood: *On the Waterfront*

that I would explain to him what I had in mind, and he would listen, but his listening was so total that it was an amazing experience to talk to him: he would not answer right away, but go away and then do something that often surprised me. You had a feeling of 'God, that's better than what I told him!' You had a feeling 'Oh, I'm so grateful to him for doing that!' He was, like, giving you a gift. It was essentially what you'd asked him, but in feeling so *true*, so re-experienced through his own artistic mechanism. It's almost like directing a genius animal. You put things in him and then you wait, you have to wait, as if it's going to hibernate or something; and then it comes out later. I don't know, I'm describing it externally. But he has everything. He has terrific feeling and violence, he has great intelligence, he's extremely intuitive. He is bisexual in the way an artist should be: he sees things both as a man and as a woman. He's strong in his sympathies to people, to all small people on the set. He's a very honest man, in that he speaks plainly to you. He's also a very devious man, in that he conceals his processes and reactions; they're none of your business. He even surprises the other actors. Sometimes you don't even know that he's acting: he does something and you say: 'Oh yes, he is! He is doing it!' He's very, very underground – you don't know *how* he gets to what he gets. Part of it is intuition, part of it is real intelligence, part of it is ability to be empathic – that he connects with the people. If the role is within his range, which is large, nobody can compare with him.

The first play he was in was something I produced – Harold Clurman directed it. He only had a three- or four-minute scene but he was marvellous. I called up Tennessee Williams, who had given me *Streetcar Named Desire*, and I said to him: 'I think I know the actor who should play Stanley Kowalski. He's young for it, but I'd like to send him up.' I said to myself, Tennessee won't like him, because he's too young, he looks like a gentle boy, although he's got strong shoulders. I got hold of Brando and I said: 'Here's twenty dollars to pay your bus fare to Boston, and from Boston to Cape Cod. Go up there.' He took the money, said 'Thank you', and left. I called Tennessee Williams the next day and said: 'Well, what did you think of him?' and he said: 'Who?' Brando had never shown up! I called him the next day and said: 'Did you like him?' and Williams said: 'Who? Nobody's come up here at all.' The third day he called me and said: 'Boy, that's it! I love him. That's the part.' I said: 'What happened?' He said: 'Well, twenty dollars is a lot of money for him. He hitch-hiked up here so he could keep the twenty dollars!' He was living that way, living around – so I'd heard – in different girls' apartments, rent-free. After that, for about three or four years, ours was a terribly close relationship. I was like his father. He used to come up here and play with my son Chris when he was a little boy. Then, when I testified, he got cool to me, but he was ambivalent. On the one hand he was grateful to me, he loved me. He told me, when he didn't do *The Arrangement*, 'You're the only director I've ever worked with' – you know, he gave me all that; and I told him, 'You're the best actor I ever worked with, too,' and he embraced me, and then he kissed me! And we parted. Still, he had this feeling of anger at me – the way a son does. A son has finally to kill his father, doesn't he? I was close to Jimmy Baldwin once too, he was like my son, I looked after him, and he watched me, and I was friendly with him. Then, all of a sudden ... I had given an idea for a play about Malcolm X, worked on it with him, really gave him some good ideas

– he called up one day and said, 'I can't do it with you.' I said, 'What's the matter?' He said: 'I want to see if I can do something on my own. You're like my father. I don't want to do it.' So that was the end of that. But it's funny, people's relationship to me: some handle it, some don't, sometimes I can handle it, sometimes I can't . . .

*Waterfront has some of the best scenes in this first part of your career: on the roof, or the scene between Steiger and Brando in the car; but the end of the film is over-directed.*

Perhaps. Possibly I over-exploited the end. My first wife used to say that when I felt uncertain about a scene, I would make it more forceful. That's been true. 'I'm uncertain, therefore you *must* believe this.' I would contest with you the idea of the scene, which is right for me; but I do agree with you that I shot it too insistently. Now I would make the longshoremen going back to work more scraggly. It looked like an army, but I would make it less cohesive. I think the music hurt that picture, Bernstein's a brilliant guy, but – you remember, the film opens with a kind of drumbeat which puts it right away on a level of melodrama, rather than just showing the murder, the body falling, just showing it – it's strong enough by itself.

Also the secondary characters were more social masks than people, and they were presented for vividness, rather than the camera just passing by them as part of life on the docks.

The photography was superb. I can't say too much good about Boris Kaufman. I think he's a real artist. He looks frail, but he was very, very strong on that picture. The picture was made in hardship. It was close to zero often, and not only that, but the wind was coming in off the Hudson River and sometimes I had to go into the hotel myself and take Brando by the arm and pull him out. A lot of the actors just huddled around barrels in which fires were burning at all times – they're shown in the picture, by the way. The New York skyline looked like the real thing, never picturesque in the wrong way; always grimy, it always had fabric to it.

In *On the Waterfront* we had a beginning crew, a crew that had not worked together. They were not coherent, and they were not very friendly towards Boris; I was protecting him all the time. They disliked him – he was a foreigner, he seemed to fumble; he didn't express himself in a forthright manner, but like an artist, in subtle things. This annoyed the fellows who had come out of television and commercials, mostly. I thought, well, Kaufman is the best cameraman I've ever got, so I'm going to stay with him. I did *Baby Doll* with him. In that film, I thought, the photography was even better.

*Spiegel was a great constructionist, at that time.*

I thought so, yes. He helped with the script a lot. He taught me a lesson – never to be satisfied with the script that you have. He said a wonderful thing that I never forgot: 'Let's open it up again.' By which he meant: 'Let's open our minds again to a basically different construction, let's keep our minds open.' In time I augmented this: 'If you feel something is wrong, admit it yourself.'

Spiegel worked on the script month after month. He drove Schulberg crazy. Schulberg got up one night, in the middle of the night – he was living in Pennsylvania then; and his second wife saw him in the bathroom at 3 a.m., shaving, and she said: 'What are you doing shaving at three in the morning?' He said: 'I'm going to New York to kill Spiegel.' He was shaving himself, and he got dressed, and he went to New York; he wanted to kill Spiegel, because Spiegel kept saying: 'It's very good now, I think we've got it. Let's start casting; all right.' And then the next day he'd say: 'Let's talk about this again, let's open it up again.' Schulberg thought Spiegel changed his mind because he'd had other people reading the script and making suggestions – probably Spiegel had. He annoyed me too, except that later I felt: well, he's right. I think he contributed an enormous amount to that film. There's an interesting gossip story about Zanuck and *On the Waterfront* that I ought to tell you, too.

Schulberg and I worked with Zanuck for a while on *On the Waterfront*. Fox was going to do it, and we worked four or five months on it. We went out to California to show Zanuck the result of our work. I'd become disillusioned with Zanuck, I wanted to get out of there anyway; but I owed him a picture by contract. Zanuck said: 'I don't want to do this picture. Who the hell gives a shit about labour unions?' After that meeting I got into his Cadillac limousine with my agent, and my agent said: 'What are you going to do next?' which meant he'd given up. I said: 'I'm going to do this picture, in 16mm, if necessary. I'm going to make it like a home movie, but I'm going to do it.' I was mad at my agent, I was mad at Hollywood, I was mad at everybody in those days. Spiegel was at a low point in his career at that time. In fact, his difficulties were so bad that he was forced to do a picture, and I think ours was the only picture he could get. He turned out tremendous as far as helping us went.

*The scene with the pigeons is the first lyrical love scene you have in your films.*

I think the reason I had so much feeling then was that I was being so criticised by old friends; and my wife was so true and loving, all through that experience ... I think people grow through pain and difficulties. I'm talking about artists, I'm not talking about architects or people who design and build cars, or farmers.

I guess the success of *Waterfront* was one of the happiest moments in my life. After *Man on a Tightrope* closed – it had one of the lowest grosses in Hollywood history – I was *persona non grata* among the intellectuals, *persona non grata* everywhere. I was nothing. The sense of triumph I had when we got the Academy Award for a New York picture made inexpensively by a lot of people like Spiegel, who was a clown, and I, who was *persona non grata*, and Budd, who wasn't anything much then either – the fact that we beat them all – was a great pleasure to me!

Terry Malloy felt as I did. He felt ashamed and proud of himself at the same time. He wavered between the two, and he also felt hurt by the fact that people – his own friends – were rejecting him. He also felt that it was a necessary act. He felt like a fool, but proud of himself because he found out that he was better than the other people around him. That kind of ambivalence. It wasn't as deep as what comes later, where everything is ambivalent. Terry's considered a hoodlum – that has a personal element, because I was considered a rough boy. I wasn't thought much of when I was young either. I always thought my father preferred my younger brother to me; he always called my younger brother 'sweet Abie', and I felt he disapproved of me and was disappointed in me, all my life, because I wouldn't go into the rug business. This is partly imaginary, because he probably liked me. I dunno, I can't tell now; it's too late to find out.

*The character of the priest is too dominant – and the ending looks*

Kazan (right) with Budd Schulberg during the shooting of *A Face in the Crowd*

*almost like a crucifixion, like a Christian ending. The social criticism is undermined by this symbolism.*

I can see your point and though I don't agree I'm not going to contest it. I did another thing that people took as symbolic. I guess it was. You know, when the bald-headed longshoreman gets killed, down in the hold, they put him on a rack; and the priest stands there, and some people have said his soul is rising to heaven. But that's the way you get out of the hold of a boat; there's no other way. There's a narrow little iron staircase that you climb up but you can't climb up with a dead body. But they said no, it's the priest taking his soul up to heaven. The fact is, I'm not in the least religious.

*Three years later, you made your second film with Budd Schulberg.*

We approached *A Face in the Crowd* like *On the Waterfront*, like people who are determined to know a subject thoroughly. We wanted to work together again because we had a good friendship, worked well together and felt very quick to understand each other, 'in tune', very *simpático*. We were looking around for a subject, and Budd suggested I read a short story of his. It was much more satirical than the movie finally was. We decided to do it, and he got a house in Connecticut, about a mile and a half down the road and moved in with his family for the whole summer. Then we began to do research, the way you would for a book on economics or history or an exposé of the automobile industry. We went to advertising agencies and to the place where the story takes place: Piggott, Arkansas. We agreed on a basic outline, which was not hard, because we see life and things the same way.

Then we separated. I did *Cat on a Hot Tin Roof* on the stage and he wrote a first draft based on our plans. Then we began to plan the production together. I suggested some rewriting to strengthen the script. It was an ideal relationship and I urged him to be around every day we were shooting. Then I edited and at the end of the cutting, he was back again and we discussed it. It was a totally collaborative effort, even down to the book for which I wrote the preface. Theoretically, I think one man should make a picture. But in the rare case where an author and a director have had the same kinds of experience, have the same kind of taste, the same historical and social point of view, and are as compatible as Budd and I are, it works out perfectly.

*You made most of* Face in the Crowd *on location.*

We became acquainted with a community of strangers – it was not like a work experience, it was a life experience, a thing that affects you very deeply. We became part of that Arkansas community settling down in new homes there. It was a terrific experience, right from the beginning, the people we met, the insights we got, the privilege we had of being inside a society that otherwise we would never have touched. We met the Governor of Arkansas, we met the mayor of this town, we met everybody in this town. Everywhere I walked, in Piggott, people were following me. It was like we had the whole town under the reverse of martial law! As though we had liberated the whole town. Like the American troops coming into a small village south of Paris. People ran up to us and spoke to us . . .

We cast many people from Nashville; Lonesome Rhodes's friend who twitches his toes, he's from the Grand Ole Opry, a regular comedian there. We went around a lot of clubs, picking up entertainers. I had heard Andy Griffith on a record, then I saw him on TV. In most ways he did very well in the part. What he did especially well was what I saw in him first. He was the real native American country boy and that comes over in the picture. I had him drunk all through the last big scene because it was the only way he could be violent – in life he wants to be friends with everybody.

*You went to Madison Avenue?*

They let us into meetings though they knew we were going to write on it. We saw the product discussions, we saw the charts. Everything that's in that picture, we have an example for. We watched many sessions on the selling of Lipton's tea, the discussions of the word 'brisk' and how to picturise it. The key word is brisk – Lipton's tea is brisk. That's not a word that affects me very strongly, but apparently they had success with the word. The discussions were really ludicrous; you could hardly keep a straight face at them. But as well as the ridiculous side, you could feel the intense, neurotic pressure they all worked under. We also went to Washington – we saw Lyndon Johnson, by the way, we talked to him for half an hour and asked him some questions pertaining to the last quarter of the story, the part that has to do with politics. He was impressed, I think, with the fact that Hollywood people were talking to him. The film, though, was organised out of my little office in New York. The crew worked out of there. We went on location from New York to Arkansas. And then we hired a big studio in the Bronx, the old Gold Medal Studio where Griffith and Ince made a lot of pictures in the old days.

*It is the only film where you deal directly with politics, from Piggott, Arkansas, to Washington D.C. Your other films are infused with politics.*

One of the points we wanted to make with the picture was the fantastic upward mobility in this country, the speed with which a man goes up and goes down. That we both knew well, because we'd both been up and down a few times. It's best illustrated in the film when he goes down in the elevator. We were thinking of suicide at one time, but we abandoned it. Budd had been impressed with a picture his father had made with a German actor about a king or a prime minister left all alone in his castle and who at the end was screaming for everybody to come back.

We were talking about the danger of power in the television medium; you can look at an audience and smile at them and win them with your smile, not with your thoughts, with your personality, not with your deeds. We weren't dealing with power abstractly, with the fact that power corrupts people, but with the fact that power is attainable in a new way that makes it especially dangerous.

*Was Lonesome scheming from the beginning, or just naïve?*

Neither. I don't think he was scheming. He always enjoyed playing with people and seducing them. And he was always related to people in a double way, or a tricky way. He lived by his wits. He was scheming in that sense. But he was also fired with a truthfulness which was the ambiguity of his character and which we perhaps didn't get enough of in the production. Even in his worst moments, he should have been saying things that nobody else saw or said. He should have had some more brilliance or honest perceptions – even at the end.

There was something about him that was down-to-earth truthful. He saw the truth and said it right away. And there was the real source of his power. The real source of his power was not his trickiness but his knack of seeing something that everybody feels but doesn't dare say, and he dares say it; or something everybody's afraid of, and he takes a stand against it, and they think they need him. We thought of a man who had great attraction, great potential, and great danger. We made fun of him a little bit too much, and except at the beginning didn't show his strength or his appeal to human beings.

Our basic interest in this picture was Lonesome Rhodes as a legend. It was to make a legendary figure of him, and to warn the public: look out for television. Remember, this was Eisenhower's time, and Eisenhower won the elections because everybody looked at him and said: 'There's Grandpa!' We're trying to say: never mind what he looks like, never mind what he reminds you of, listen to what he's saying! I was trying (and I didn't quite succeed) to make Lonesome Rhodes walk a tightrope, so you'd feel: 'Jesus Christ, *I would* give in to that man!' And, at the same time, 'If I gave in to that man, it would be a disaster.' I think I let the audience off too easily, in a position where they could patronise him, where they could look down on him, and say: 'Oh, those jackasses! How could they be taken in by that man!' But they shouldn't feel that. They should say: 'I could be taken in.' It left them in a safe position. I think that's the single failure of the film.

We were also saying, however, that television is a good thing. Abraham Lincoln said: 'Tell the people the truth, and they will decide what to do.' Well, we said that television is good for that – it's a better way. Television deludes some people, exposes others. What interested us in the character of Marcia was that after she learned and knew for sure that Lonesome was a no-good, she still couldn't resist him. That's very much part of the legend of Hollywood; it's full of attractive, cruel, sadistic but sexy bastards. It's Pygmalion in reverse. I guess, since she made him, she had to stay with him.

This film *was* in advance of its time. It foretells Nixon. I don't think it was about McCarthy particularly. I think it would have been better if we had had a political figure in the Senator who could conceivably have won an election. Our senator, you feel, is such an ass, that you never think he might. I think we made fools of the side we didn't like. Marshall Neilan, the former director, played the part and he couldn't remember a word – he was terrified. He was so grateful, he'd been out of films for so many years and that made him nervous. It was sad and very touching.

Patricia Neal and Andy Griffith in *A Face in the Crowd*

*It is your most misanthropic film.*

Possibly. I was conscious of it. But I really thought that's the way that world was – the advertising world. Here and there, there are decent people, but they're all under such pressure, they all live in such fear of losing their jobs, that it tends to become that way. The journalist played by Walter Matthau was not dealt with mercifully. I've never been very favourably inclined towards 'intellectuals'. I mean – I like *intellect*. But the intellectuals around New York who sit and complain about why they're not doing things, and a lot of the intellectuals I know from the progressive movements at various times – I dunno, maybe some of that got in there. Budd thinks that character *is* sympathetic. I don't think he has much gumption, or strength.

*The hysteria is more carefully controlled than in* On the Waterfront.

I think it's done better and there's a lot of humour in it. I've never

Lonesome Rhodes endorses the product but later shatters the myth of his own infallible judgment

done anything as funny as this. The majorettes . . . Lee Remick was marvellous. She went there three weeks ahead, she lived with a family in the town, trained with the local high school's majorettes.

*You are less satisfied with the second part of* A Face in the Crowd?

I learned a lesson about style in that film. Thornton Wilder used to tell me: 'The hidden cause, the concealed cause, of most of the serious trouble with good scripts is the mixture of styles.' It's the most difficult thing to catch, and you can delude yourself. He told me that again and again, and he dealt in mixtures of styles. *The Skin of Our Teeth* could have gone off a lot because he mixed some styles, but he did it successfully. I don't know how – by making it a little grotesque, I guess.

The first part of *A Face in the Crowd* is more of a satire, and the second part tends to really involve you with Lonesome's fate and with his feelings. I think the first part works perfectly, and the second part doesn't quite. Maybe the change should have been in the first

117

part, despite the fact that it worked. If I had made him more humanly attractive, it might have been less funny, but it would have made the two parts coherent. I think this is a good example of that mixture of styles which I think is a critical point in films. When you mix styles, you're in a lot of trouble. In the beginning of a film, you are saying to an audience: 'I want you to listen to this story and take it this way.' Afterwards you can't·break it, you can't say: 'I want you to laugh at Lonesome Rhodes.' If it's a satire, you can't be terrorised emotionally later.

*Why do you think entertainers seek power?*

In the first place, they deal with power. Their power is with an audience. When they step in front of the audience at the Grand Ole Opry, there are five thousand people sitting there who start to run up and want to touch them and follow them in the streets. They're offered money and that's power, isn't it? And they feel it and enjoy it. They have this magical thing, confidence, or beauty, or talent that people are attracted to. Billy Graham and Huey Long were models for the character. And Arthur Godfrey, definitely. But Huey Long did a lot of good in Louisiana. He was basically a tyrant, but he got many, many reforms; and he was genuinely interested, at the beginning, in the problems of the poor. Lonesome Rhodes should have been more like him, more genuinely interested in the poor.

*Why wasn't the film successful? How were the reviews?*

They were pretty good. I don't know why it didn't go. We said: 'Oh, they're not ready for it,' and in a way they weren't. We said: 'Oh, they don't want us to criticise America,' and in a way they didn't. And we said: 'Oh, they think we are communists, and putting America down, trying to destroy America,' and we were attacked some for that. But I think a picture that tries to do something as difficult as this picture has to be perfect and I don't think we were, not quite. There was a great gaiety, making up those ads, the Vitajex sequence . . . I was both repulsed and attracted by them. TV is always on the verge of being ludicrous, it's always on the precipice – and you say, 'I can't believe they mean that! Are they kidding?' What I like in the film is the energy and invention and bounce which are very American. It's really got something marvellous about it, this constantly flashing, changing rhythm. In many ways, it's more American than any picture I ever did. It represents the business life, and the urban life, and the way things are on television, the rhythm of the way this country moves. It has a theme that even today is completely relevant. Finally what I think is that it was ahead of its time.

# 8: Colour and Wide Screen: *East of Eden* (1955), *Wild River* (1960), *Splendor in the Grass* (1961)

*The only time you went back to Hollywood was for the first film that you produced:* East of Eden.

That film was made partly in northern California, partly in the studio. After *On the Waterfront*, I could have everything; any story, any power, any money. I said to myself: Just make your own scripts from now on. Steinbeck, as I told you, was a close friend ... He brought out this book, *East of Eden*, and I found something in the end of it, in the last eighty pages, that I liked as film material.

*Viva Zapata!* had been a collaboration. I had provided the basic structure and John the knowledge of the character, the background, and the way they spoke. I often would say a line and John would say: 'Okay.' I often would say: 'The next scene should be —' and John would say: 'Okay.' John was also thinking of a next book, and I sat at the typewriter in his room and typed that script out. I would say it was an equal collaboration, although the credits don't say anything about me. I was very careful in those days, because if you say you're collaborating, writers won't want to work with you because, they say, you're moving in on them. When I got through with *Viva Zapata!*, I felt I didn't know as much about structure as I should. Particularly, I found that *Viva Zapata!* had a diffuseness about it. I didn't want that; I wanted to get more unity in my subjects. I asked John if it was all right if I got another writer and John said sure, fine.

I got Paul Osborn because I think he's an excellent constructionist and still a very adaptable man. He listens, when you don't like something, and changes it. He doesn't get up on his ego and say: 'That's the way it is,' the way Robert Sherwood did with me. He is

*East of Eden*: Abra (Julie Harris) watches Cal (James Dean) smash the ice in his father's new storeroom

gentle, and understanding. I wanted him to provide a unity of structure that I felt I was not yet able to provide for myself. About five or six years later, I found that it was better to have more of my own statements and my own life, and a little less unity, because the unity, I began to find, simplifies things too much. Sometimes it simplifies the life out of things, and makes them too clear. Osborn and I worked in a room, here in Connecticut. We'd talk about a scene, and he'd go home and write it, and the next day he'd bring it back. Piece by piece, day by day.

In that story, of course, what attracted me was nothing very mysterious: the story of a son trying to please his father who disapproved of him was one part of it. Another part of it was an opportunity for me to attack puritanism; the absolute puritanism of 'this is right and this is wrong'. I was trying to show that right and wrong get mixed up, and that there are values that have to be looked at more deeply than in that absolute approval-or-disapproval syndrome of my Left friends. Those two elements, I think, are in that film. There's the

121

girl who understands the bad boy, when no one else does, like in *On the Waterfront.*

When I was young, I was full of anger. I looked like a hungry wolf; I was thin, my eyes were close together and I wouldn't look at anybody. I look at pictures of myself then, and I can see the resentment, the hatred towards everybody. And my first wife saw the good in me, and she was sympathetic to me – when we were young, and first together, and first married, and had children, it was a blessing that she did that for me. The gentleness and understanding that Julie Harris has in that film was very much taken out of the gentleness and understanding that my wife had for me. It didn't last long – only five or six years – but maybe nothing like that can last long because I developed one way and she developed another. It was autobiographical, that picture – more personal than anything I've ever done. There's some disguise, some transfers, but I knew every feeling in that picture. That's why it is very pure. You like it or you don't, but what's being said there is heartfelt. That was the first picture, I feel, that started this talking about myself through film-making.

*The very size of CinemaScope prevented you from doing too many close-ups, as in* Man on a Tightrope *or some scenes of* On the Waterfront. *It forced you to be more simple.*

As I studied films, in *Panic in the Streets*, and studied Ford, and began to think more theoretically about films, leading up to *On the Waterfront* (including the circus picture), I made up my mind that films are essentially an art of cutting. In other words, no shot has a significance by itself; it gets significance by what it's next to and what it follows. That was the theory I had then. Now, without my thinking too much about it, the CinemaScope made it impossible to cut as often. The face didn't fill the screen so I did a staging that was much more relaxed, more like a stage – more 'across', more at ease. It was not intentional; I was forced into it by the aesthetics of that shape. I also did something else; I combated the shape, I tried to get inner frames. In other words, I would put something big in the foreground on one side, something black, that you couldn't see through, and put the action on the other side. The next time I'd have the action in a corner over there, and have something blocking it here. I tried to make frames within the frame. In Kate's house, for instance, everything is black and out of focus except the corridor, which by the way I shouldn't have put right in the middle but on the side of the frame.

I tried to make an asset of my problem; but I never liked the CinemaScope frame. I think one-six-six is a pretty good ratio. I actually prefer the old size still better because I like the depth, and I like cutting. I still feel that, basically. But I don't cut insistently any more. I would do a film, though, in any shape, depending on the subject. I think it's one of your means and there should not be any set shape.

*It was your first use of colour and it goes with the lyricism and the gentleness.*

I approached it like a demon. You know, I was determined that I would get good colour, and I didn't like other people's colour at all. And I had a colour plot. I think the best colour I ever had was at the end of *East of Eden*. That room is so green and so dark, where he dies, that you feel something poetic about that scene, that you wouldn't have if it had been in black and white, or in ordinary colours, a cream-coloured room or a light room ... I worked that colour out with extreme care. And I used a lot of greens. Everybody said: don't use green, green comes out black, you can't light green, green eats the light ... There's a lot of green in that picture. And I thought, it's verdant, it's a valley – and Steinbeck's description of Salinas: green, green, green. The old man dies in green: a death's version of his valley, that was the idea.

Anyway, I worked it out carefully, and I had help on that from a wonderful cameraman, Ted McCord, a terrific, mean old man. People didn't like to work with him. He was pigheaded, bullheaded. But boy, when you talked to him, he *worked*. He really tried to give you his equivalent for what you wanted. He had a lot of guts. I got Ted because I liked *Treasure of the Sierra Madre* which he had photographed.

*The scenes between Julie Harris and James Dean have the lyricism of* On the Waterfront.

I think his face was very poetic, I think his face was wonderful and very painful. You really feel so sorry for him when you see him in close-up; but I realised there was great value in his body. His body was more expressive, actually, in free movement, than Brando's – it had so much tension in it. Brando has terrific tension, but he has

123

great strength in being static. And his movements are wonderful – Brando's a genius. But Dean had a very vivid body; and I did play a lot with it in long shots. And CinemaScope emphasised Dean's smallness. When he runs in the bean fields; there's a big thing like that, wide, and you see Dean running through it, looking like a little child. I also like the scene under the tree; the tree is a willow, and the branches fall down and are covering Dean and Julie. That's an adolescent dream: to get under and cuddle with a girl, and you're alone in the world.

Julie Harris was wonderful. I wanted to make it so that her face, what's in her face, is the key to the picture; because her face has in it the feeling I had towards the characters, of compassion and understanding of pain. Her face is the most compassionate face of any girl I've ever seen, and I stressed it. I contrasted her face and Massey's, which was a piece of wood.

*You had more complex camera movements than in your previous films, as in the scenes at the fair or when Massey sees the train leaving.*

Oh yes, that was my movement. I liked that. What happens is: the train starts, and there's a lot of movements; then the camera pans to a house, and there's nobody in front of the house, it's silent and stationary; and the camera goes by this house, there's no movement; then it goes a little further, and in the distance you see the train going.

I was getting more enjoyment, pleasure, artistic release. In *On the Waterfront* I kept the camera nailed down. Here I was beginning to deal with poetry. *Waterfront* has some poetry in the photography, and *Zapata* has some poetry too, but not where I expected. Anyway, I knew *East of Eden* was a small, tender, poetic story. And John's descriptions of scenery are the best of any American writer, better than Faulkner, better than Hemingway.

I love the country in the morning. I love the leaves; that's one reason I get up early. But John even more. He was brought up in nature – I wasn't. I came to it late in my life. I idealise the country. I think we're being squeezed to death. That's why I regard the super highways they're building here as threats. I can't go by them without thinking of them symbolically. I'm on a committee to stop them and I have great antagonism towards the suburbanisation of American life.

Abra welcomes Cal's father (Raymond Massey) to his surprise birthday party

Everything'll be a suburb, the way cities are despoiled and vulgarised.

*There's also a great deal of humour, and fun. I think* Eden *is the first film in which you have a lighter touch.*

Yes, I do feel that. I had affection for the subject. My emotions in *Waterfront* were anger, hatred. Even in *Zapata*: anger at injustice, anger at hatred. But this was the first film in which I opened up and allowed myself to experience the emotion of tenderness and lovingness towards other people. Julie Harris embodied this feeling, released the love potential in Dean so that it could be exercised – she began to make a loving person of him. The failure in this picture is Massey's character which I could have done better. I think I was cruel to him and made him like a stock. There *are* moments when you feel for Massey, when his poor wooden face stands there and the water is leaking from the cars and he doesn't respond to it.

You have to forgive your father, finally. You have to say: 'Well, I don't like you for this, and I don't like you for that,' but if you continue to live in that hate, you don't grow up. I've always believed that hate destroys the hater. The thing to do is have compassion for everybody. That's what I admire about Tolstoy. He sees all sides of everything. I love that, that's my goal, that's what I'd like to do. I can't do it yet, but maybe before I die I'll do it a couple of times. Compassion for everybody.

Also, I did feel I treated the younger brother badly. I should have done better with that. I put him down. Those are the faults of the picture. I'm not crazy about the character of the mother either. Women like that did exist, prosper, and behave very tightly and puritanically. What Cal feels in her is a tolerance of the evil that's in people, a tolerance of the non-puritanical elements. *I* think she's very puritanical. I think she's still, rigid, very judgmental and bigoted. I think she's a victim too, just like the father. I think they're both social products – products of the West.

What Dean is saying is simply that 'You, father, feel that you must have money, for whatever reasons. By whatever means, I will get you what you feel you need.' He also feels poignantly towards his father, because his father is incapable of doing that. He feels the world is just a tough world, and in some way or other, he'll get it. That's all against the background of the war, which made million-aires in this country through what we used to call 'profiteering'. Fortunes were made in corrupt ways during the war – like what they did with the beans, by buying something in advance for such-and-such a figure, and then they'd get a much bigger figure. The country was fighting so that democracy would live, and at the same time it was being corrupted by the money philosophy that it lived under. All Dean was doing in that picture was saying: 'You're up against a tough racket, Daddy; and I'll play the racket for once, I'll get you the money for once,' but it doesn't imply that he becomes that way. I never intended that.

*But the 'good guy' is also trying to deprive his brother of his father's affection.*

Yes, and he's jealous of it, and also he tries, in effect, to kill his brother, by putting him down. Also, there's some judgment I make in there that goodness is sterile: I don't agree. I think there are 'good' people who are not sterile, who are not cruel. But I don't know if that's within the scope of this story. This film is terribly autobiographical in its feelings. I felt people had been right to hate me in 1951, but I mustn't hate them. I must forget it and go on with my life. I must also forgive my father, I must write a book called *America America* about my father and understand why he became that way, why Greeks are crafty and hidden, why Jews feel outsiders all the time. I have to rid myself of hate. See, I have been psychoanalysed. And one of the things I learned was not to blame other people for my problems but to look at myself. One of the most important things you learn in psychoanalysis is when you start saying: 'But my wife did this, but my father did that,' the analyst, if he's any good, turns you around and says: 'Yes, but what did *you* do?'

*When were you psychoanalysed?*

I was twice. The first one wasn't much help. It started in 1945, because I had left my wife and I still loved her. I'd left her and I was living with another girl in California; and although I loved her in many ways, too – I realised that you can love two women at once, or three; you can love a lot of people – I was also unhappy, and I missed my children and my wife. And I decided to leave this other girl and go back to my wife. Then I began to be psychoanalysed so I could find out who I was, and what I felt; but it didn't help much. I couldn't explain to him that deep in my heart I was dissatisfied with my life. That success didn't mean anything to me. So I finally said: this man is trying to make me adjust to a society, a state of affairs, that I don't like. I went further: I said, anyone who adjusts to this society is a bastard. Anyone who says you should live and be happy within the society is no good. And I quit the man.

I was really psychoanalysed in 1959, before *Splendor in the Grass*. I went to the man and I said to him: 'I want you to be tough. Don't tell me I'd get along; I don't want to. I want to write my own stories, I want to write books, I want to write my own films. And something is preventing me from doing it, some lack of confidence, some lack of belief in myself. That's what I'm here for. Don't tell me I'm a famous director and have money in the family and all that. I don't care about those things.' And, due to my work with him, I wrote *America America*. *The Arrangement* is full of psychoanalysis. Although I make fun of it, the book is in praise of psychoanalysis, the book is a concealed psychoanalysis, through the action of the man. That second psychoanalysis affected my whole life.

*Wild River* took several years to prepare.

For this film, I have to go way back. When I was a communist, in 1934–35, I used to go to Tennessee, as I told you, and visit a man in Chatanooga who was head of the communist unit there, a fellow I liked very much. It was the time of Roosevelt, the TVA was just being built and I got an idea about a film twenty-five years before I actually made it. In 1941, when I was working on *It's Up to You*, my formal employment came from the Department of Agriculture where many men were either in tune with Roosevelt or continuing the New Deal policies. I became interested in the TVA because the Department of Agriculture liberals were all involved in it.

Later, around 1955, I read a book by William Bradford Huie, *Mud in the Stars*, which involved the TVA. We bought the other book, by Borden Deal, which is on the credits, so that somebody else wouldn't buy it and make a film about it. Very little of it was used, just atmosphere. Then I began to think it was about time I tried to write my own scripts. I wrote that script at least three times. A few of the scenes were used in the movie but not many. I had trouble organising the material into any kind of compressed or unified form. Why so many years between these first scripts of mine and the shooting? There were two reasons: first, I was alternately failing at creating a script that I liked and resisting the idea of getting someone else to work on it, because I'd made up my mind to write myself. But, in order to keep busy or 'continue my prestigious career', I was doing plays. That took up a lot of time.

*At one time you were thinking of Robert Ardrey for the script.*

He would have been a good choice for it, because he is also very close to me. Our friendship survived two plays that failed, which is not usual. We keep up a connection. I try to keep as many friendships, acquaintances, contacts going as I possibly can. I have friends all over the world, and I follow their course, I follow their changes, I follow their fates, all over. I believe in that too, but I'm not close, too close, to anybody.

130

*After you, Ben Maddow, Calder Willingham, and finally Paul Osborn worked on the script. Do you think simplicity requires more effort?*

Yes, I do. You know Lord Chesterfield's famous letter to his son: 'Excuse me for writing a long letter. I didn't have time to write a short one.' Whenever you write a script, it's very hard to cut it within the first month. You have to get some distance so that it is not your thing that you're defending, but someone else's and you can get some objectivity. So you take Maddow and you say: 'Come on, Ben, write on this subject.' So he reads it, thinks about it, talks to you, then he finally starts to work, does some research, and he finally writes it – that's nine months gone! Then you read Maddow's script; another month goes. You think about it – how the hell am I going to tell Maddow I don't like it? You finally tell him: 'Ben, I don't like it. I'd like to try it myself.' Then you write the version yourself, and that takes six months. All the time all this was going on, I was doing those plays.

As I remember my script, what was kept was the basic concept of the woman on the island. The island was going to be inundated, she resisted it and was finally overcome. Those are good and solid elements. My hero was a Jew. The Jew was all right with Ben Maddow, but not particularly good for Calder Willingham, and all right for me, but not good for Paul Osborn. Paul Osborn describes every leading man like he's Henry Fonda. Henry Fonda comes off his typewriter naturally. So the first thing he says is: 'I'd like to make him . . . a regular guy, a guy we know well.' *We* – you mean, *him!* He wanted to call him 'Chuck Glover' or something like that. That's how that started. And I didn't resist it at all, because Paul was comfortable in that milieu. Then I thought about it and I said to myself, well, there's justice in what Paul is doing, because the other conflict is a mechanical one: Jew *vs.* Gentile. It's too obvious; it's even a cliché. So Jews and Gentiles don't get along – bullshit!

But making Chuck Glover a Gentile was immediately to make the conflicts on the basis of city *vs.* country, intellectual *vs.* uneducated, bureaucrat *vs.* emotionally committed peasants. And that's much deeper and much more real, and it's the conflict of the story – not New York City Jew *vs.* a country person. Then, I did an awful lot of research, a lot of walking around, taking holidays there. I was chased off several places where I worked – they didn't like my looks. When

131

they got to know me, they liked me, but when they first saw me they said: 'There's a New York Kike come down here to make trouble.'

I meant to make it as good a picture as I could, and I never realised it would be as simple as it turned out to be. Only after I'd sweated through all my versions was I ready to say: this should be simple – a basic, primitive, Biblical story – you can't embroider it, Kazan, so just tell! It took time for me to get that. *Wild River* shouldn't be overcrowded, it shouldn't be full of effects, it should just be telling my own love affair with the New Deal; my love affair with the people in the back parts of this country – how much I love and admire them. That's the first time I use the word, my loving my material. In the next four films I did, it became so more and more. I learned a lot, again, and that simplicity helped me later with *America America*, because whatever else *America America* has, the story is Biblical, fundamental. We all search for this: a story that contains its theme within itself, without having to state it constantly. *Wild River* and *America America* came closest to my theory of the humble and the poetic, the unnoticed poetry that's all around us: *Wild River* was never even shown anywhere. All kinds of pictures are being revived, but not *Wild River*. I asked to buy it but Fox wants 300,000 dollars which I can't give them. Out of my last eight pictures, I had six colossal disasters, the exceptions being *East of Eden* and *Splendor in the Grass*, so what do you expect them to feel about me? I'm someone that's going to bankrupt their company.

*Originally Chuck Glover was the same age (25) as you were during the New Deal.*

The truth is that I was looking to make it that way. The training of an actor is useful in one sense to a director: you try to find yourself in the role, you try to find the role in yourself. And this role was no problem, because I said, well, this is the way I was then. I was shy, uncertain with girls – like almost everybody is. In that film, I tried to make everything as close as I could, I moved everything to myself. I knew the experience there, I didn't have to deal with it abstractly. I took him from myself, because I knew what my own weaknesses were, which are not the same weaknesses I have now. But I also took him from a model in the Dept. of Agriculture. I knew my boss for instance, he was one thing in the office, and at night when he got drunk and played music and talked to me, he was another man. He

Mob violence directed at Montgomery Clift and Lee Remick in *Wild River*

revealed all his weaknesses. I felt there are two sides to that kind of bureaucrat, the official side and the personal side; and the personal side is often affronted by the necessity of the official side presenting a strong façade. But I try not to do that in an exposing way, though sometimes I can't help it. I try to be critical but loving, privately uncertain, with my characters.

*You had worked with Clift on the stage in* The Skin of Our Teeth.

For the film I found him in terrible shape. He's dead now, so I can say it. I loved Monty Clift. I had a relationship with him like with Brando; he used to come to my house and tell me his problems, and my wife was sort of a mother-figure to him. He had a terrible set of neurotic problems. Sometimes you couldn't even look at him, he was in such pain.

I resisted getting Monty Clift because I didn't think he had the strength to do it. I wouldn't have taken him if I could've had Brando; and then finally I went ahead with him. Before the film he was drunk, all the time. I said to him: 'Monty, you must give me your word of

133

honour that you won't take one drink during this production.' Well, that's a very hard thing to ask a drinker; he can't stop quickly, he's got to taper off. But I can't work with a drunk, I have trouble working with drunks. Well, by God, during the production he got better, stronger, more confident. And then, about three days before it was over, he came on the set one day, walked up to me to say hello and fell flat on his face: he had been drinking again. His hair was getting thin and the make-up man had to put black in it. And he was terribly uncertain with girls – like a homosexual is. Lee Remick helped; it's why she comes out so strong in that film, like an aggressive woman who makes up her mind: 'He's going to marry me and I'm going to marry him. He's going to be the father of my children. I'm going to get him.' Well, that made my unbalance a little stronger, right? I mean, the casting helped give the impression that I was beating the shit out of the intellectual.

*There's a switch of the conflict: he sides with the old woman versus the men who beat him up.*

I don't know if it's a switch. I think that's dramaturgy. It's true to life. You have to say, not that he was sympathetic to her point of view, but that he's so sympathetic that he acts in her behalf. He has moved to some sort of allegiance with her. Furthermore, if I didn't make him do that, that story would be over, in the sense that he understands the opponent. The external story could stop any minute, the personal story keeps it going.

*The same composer worked on* Wild River *and on* Baby Doll.

I found Kenyon Hopkins self-effacing, and the least intrusive of my composers; the most personal and the most intrusive was Leonard Bernstein. I wouldn't ask Leonard Bernstein to do a film again for pie in the sky; if it was going to be revived at Radio City Music Hall I wouldn't have him do the film again. Not because I don't like him – I like Leonard, he's a very nice man – but he's an ego, and film music doesn't need another ego, it needs someone who helps the central ego, in achieving its maniacal, self-destructive dream! I also wanted the music to have a simple folk quality, a genuine, unadorned, unvaried quality – just like the breeze going through a picture.

*Carol is the only complete, balanced, developed human being among characters in your films. Did you feel that?*

Yes, I did. I may have idealised her a bit, but basically she is true. I felt she'd taken a lot of pain; she'd lost her husband, she had no way of making a living, she had to take care of her grandmother, she was deprived of things. And in some ways she had accepted all these difficulties and was able to go on. She hadn't married easily just to get a man, just to have a life with a man – she'd put him off, she delayed, she'd done what a woman instinctively does, saying: 'Well, I'm not sure, better not do anything.' She had a nice man – I made him nice too – Walter – so I didn't break up something bad, I broke up something nice. Ten years before I would have made him a sonofabitch of some kind, and you'd want Clift to rescue her. But you have doubts, saying, well, maybe she would have been better off with Walter. Walter was a wonderful man whereas Clift looks more neurotic, what's she going to do in Washington? You have double thoughts, the way you do in life. Sexually, I find that girls who have strength, who are nice girls, 'proper' girls – when they find a man, they go to bed with him quicker, because there's no calculation; that's it, they don't hold anything back. In other ways, she is much more uninhibited, she's natural.

She's a fifties girl in the thirties. I think another reason for her security is that she doesn't pretend to be something she's not. A lot of middle-class bourgeois girls pretend: they present themselves as having more culture, or more decency, or less aggressiveness than they actually have. They have a big mask this girl doesn't have.

*The setting in the past created a distance.*

The past remembered in tranquillity, emotion remembered in tranquillity. And it is better that way, you get a better balance. If I were to describe the fight I had with someone last month, it would all be on my side, I would be angry and so on: but I would treat that man unfairly. Also, there's something beautiful about the old that made me want to make the picture. When I was a young man I said: it's rotten, it must be destroyed, it must be wiped off the face of the earth – we have a terrible imperialist, colonialist, stinking, arrogant, cruel, sadistic civilisation – it must be eliminated from the earth! Now I look at it and say: there were great things in the past, to a certain extent. I thought a lot about Bud Lighton, the producer of *A Tree Grows in Brooklyn*. He was a very reactionary man, but a beautiful person,

Montgomery Clift returns to the unwelcoming atmosphere of his hotel: *Wild River*

and the things he liked about the past of America were the things Ford liked. And that's why Ford is a great artist, because he likes the past. He is a modern man, but he can see that those frontier values were important. And that's why I say I'm closer to Ford than to anybody – not only because of the way I shoot, that's superficial, but because I have one foot in now and one foot in the past.

*Was it the reason why Chekhov was your favourite writer?*

Dostoievsky I admire; Chekhov I envy. I envy Chekhov because the content is so compressed, perfectly chosen, and he's put in exactly the right form. It's a complete work of art in that everything is completely real – scenes are easy, natural, inevitable. To take the simplest, realest elements and find the poetry in them – that's what Chekhov does in his little milieu, in his society. Dostoievsky does one thing I aspire to: he has a serious scene that is also funny, he mixes horror and amusement. To me, he is like a torrent, almost formless. Some of it is good, some of it is not too good, but it's a torrent of talent. It skips the formal problem, which I think an artist should somehow solve. Usually when people have good form, they sacrifice something, there's something lost. I would rather have bad form and good content. But that's why I admire Chekhov so much. He has both. He's like a natural miracle. You feel the epoch dying. You feel the people that are coming up; you feel everything about them.

*You also seem to like abandoned houses, dead leaves.*

Yes, I do, and I usually burn them! Or flood them. Painful change, change that is necessary but hurts. My family lost a house, when I was a boy. And I guess when my father died we also moved out of a house. *Wild River* was also the first picture where I said to myself: I'm going to be as lyric as I can – I'm going to stop the action. You see, I always distrusted stopping the action for lyric moments. I had much more confidence after that.

I also used long shots as in the scene with them way in the back of the room, sort of in the dark, on the floor. I did that a lot, and putting a person or an object in the foreground with deep focus. That was a way of keeping it natural, although it's an unnatural technique. I'm looking at the branch behind you, and you are not in focus, despite William Wyler and Orson Welles and everybody else. It's only fifteen feet behind you, but you are a blur.

There's one influence I won't deny. The scene I remember in Dovzhenko is the scene in the forest, in *Aerograd*, when the old men yell at each other. I think that changed my life, just one scene like that where I thought a film can be both true – realistic – and completely poetic. And that became the ideal of my aesthetic – to the extent that I was conscious of my aesthetic. Suddenly you look at it and it's as plain as a loaf of bread, and it's completely poetic at the same time. It has overtones, it has suggestions, it has poetry all around it, but then, it can also be just nothing, a loaf of bread. This is what I feel when I see paintings by Cézanne: he shows you an apple, it's just an apple on a table, but it's somehow poetic. I like that.

If I tend to say 'all artists', forget it, because I don't really believe that. I don't believe *all* artists are anything. But it's true of me. That's why I like to live in the country; see, a lot of these places here where you see fields, there used to be trees, and I cut them down. I've had

137

Natalie Wood and Kazan with writer William Inge during the shooting of *Splendor in the Grass*

my hand in putting up this building. My first wife is buried here. That's the way I live. I live with my past in the present; I like my past to be in the present, not in the past. Realer to me than the future, as real as the present, so I live in the middle of it. Everything I've done is here. And it's all poetic to me, at the same time as it's real.

*How did you come to make* Splendor in the Grass?

Bill Inge and I did *Dark at the Top of the Stairs* on stage and became very good friends. I was looking for another story and the one he told me and knew from experience struck me, especially the end of it. I think that's the most mature ending I've got on any picture I ever did. When she visits him at his place, and he's married – there's something there that is so beautiful, I don't really understand it. It's beyond anything I did – it just came out. It's not a happy ending in the mythology of Hollywood but in the real terms of life it is. Also, you feel that's he's grown up, he's a fine man ... the way he treats her, and then the way he puts his arm around his wife, and the way she goes to reassure his wife that he's not alienated. That was good. That's the reason I did it.

The basic story and characters were all beautifully provided by Inge in the manuscript; and then I wrote the script. I sent it to Inge, and I said: 'Here's the script I made out of what you sent me,' which was a very rough first draft, almost like a novel, 'and now, study it and make adjustments in it.' He didn't make many; there weren't many to make. It was a pretty good job.

Another reason why I made the film was a line Bill said: 'I'd like to tell a story about how we have to forgive our parents.' Bill was in psychoanalysis then, he resented his parents, and he was right at the moment when he was forgiving them – when he saw what they were and let them go. 'I forgive you, I love you, goodbye,' that's what it was. And so, the next scene I like best is when she's come back from the institution and the mother is unpacking and she defends herself to her daughter who embraces her, and thereby discards her. If you embrace your parents and forgive them, you can step past them and forget them.

I had a lot of intimate experience with the crash. I saw many people get killed by it, and my own father had, in effect, his spirit killed by it and so had Arthur Miller's. His father was eviscerated, he was just wandering around. I saw people who committed suicide and they *were* jumping out of the windows. I saw a man's body between two buildings just as I showed Stamper in a long shot. I think the crash still haunts this country. When they talk about inflation, what they all remember is that moment when the banks were closed, when you couldn't get money, when you couldn't buy anything with a dollar.

*It is a twin film to* Wild River. *But this time the rhythm is staccato.*

The movement of the story never stops, it keeps going. Bill is a good story-teller, and I just made up my mind to never relax it. I did trim a lot so that it would just keep flowing. I guess I felt that the crash was our fate. Like a Greek play: you know what's going to happen and you watch it happen. This country was fated to go through that terrible time, and then to be reborn. People were being in difficulty, as I was, and were finding themselves and moving forward. They could not escape or do anything about their fate, because of the sins of their past. A mother committed a sin to her little girl: she had to

Deanie with the doctor (John McGovern) in *Splendor in the Grass*

pay for it. They had to pay their dues. America paid its dues, and then had to start again. And that's what Deanie and Bud do at the end: they have to start all over again.

*Bud is the opposite of Cal . . .*

He does not rebel against his father. He's more like I was. I concealed my antagonism, that's all. If my father had given me a chance, I would have tried to live up to his hopes for me, to a certain extent. I did try, I tried to be a good boy, do what he said, run his errands. He always wanted me to cut my hair and shine my shoes; I tried all that. But then after a while I just broke loose. Ginny, his sister, is a destructive force, a good destructive force. She wants to break up her society. She's a revolutionist without knowledge, without a theory, without any technique; she has no goal, and no antagonist. So she kills herself.

*Do you think she also castrates her brother?*

140

He wants his sister and his girl-friend to be pure. Well, that's another old American characteristic: that women shouldn't be aggressive, and that all women should be virgins, pure like your mother. An aggressive woman makes many American men impotent. I think it's wonderful when a woman is aggressive, I like that. I really like that best, when a woman goes after a man. I like it for myself, and I also like to show it. There's a scene where they're all under furniture covers, and Ginny's laughing and giggling and bundling up with a boy, and Bud and Deanie are sitting nervously in another chair – she's castrating him then, because he's inhibited. Inge was castrated by somebody – I don't know who, and it made him uncertain sexually.

You know what American puritanism is: a man who has a good business and makes a lot of money is somehow good. And a man who doesn't make money and is a failure in business has something wrong with his character.

*Wealth is a substitute for sex.*

That's exactly the idea. Mrs Loomis wasn't getting any sex from her husband, therefore she felt he was a weakling in every way and she had to take over the stocks, and take over for him as a man. And he was gentler and squashed, like a bug, by her. And he got fatter and fatter. Fred Stewart, who was very good, looked in the film exactly like a capon that's got fat. But I didn't show her as a villain. In both this picture and *America America*, I tried to deal with reality of the most painful and harsh kind, but still show the good side of it.

In many ways the picture treats completely conventional elements. Except it doesn't treat them conventionally. Superficially it looks like a story in one of those magazines like *Cosmopolitan* – the circus of it. It's all corn, except by the way the author and I had insight into it. We took these conventional elements – the old story of growing up – and turned them around and showed a little more of what was in them: and then they were transformed into non-conventional elements. Examining corn, we found what was true. All my pictures are corny. But the best of them, through it, come out deep. The deepest conflicts of our society are through the violent, intimate acts that are on page 4 of that awful daily newspaper, those acts where the pressure of society forces individuals to do things that are violent and final.

The corniest of them all is *Splendor in the Grass*. It is a classic

American story examined and re-experienced. That's what I admire about Ford: he went over and over the classic American story. He's the most *human* of all the American directors, including Welles and Billy Wilder, Griffith, who was another cornball – I like him too. Try to get the basic experience of yourself, and through that you might get the basic experience of your generation, of your time. In my seven or eight last films, I think you could see the spiritual history of this goddamn country.

*There is a recurrent use of the water image in* Splendor.

Purity. Sex. Again and again. Water is oblivion, water is death, water is threatening. I almost drowned once; I was scared to death, I never got over it. Perhaps that has something to do with it. It's a positive image in the sense that Stavros says in *America America*: 'America will wash me clean.' Let me tell you this: I'm an American, very American and all that, but way back I was born in Asia Minor; and I was raised in a place where there was no running water. Water was precious, water was a beautiful thing. To wash your hands in water was something nice; you did it with a pail, you did it in a basin. It was something we didn't take for granted as Americans do. Americans take everything for granted.

*Kansas is typical of the silent majority.*

It might be hard for a European to see this, but I like Kansas people, just as I like Southern people. They're very different – they're very staid, they're in terrible trouble, they're reactionary, but there's something good about them, too. They just sit on the porch and talk and laugh. They castrated their men – but the women are strong, I sort of like the women. I went out to Kansas a lot and I wanted to shoot there but it became impossible. We found good equivalents for this. Staten Island looks very much like Kansas, and we found a place on Long Island for the last scene that was exactly like Kansas. And there was so much indoors in that film that it was better to shoot in sets, which we did for about two-thirds of it. I went to a mental institution, looked at it; I also went to the high school, I stayed a couple of days, in the halls, watching; we just sat there and took notes. I found a lot of little 'business'. I did a lot of research of that kind. I went to the place where they pump oil, in Tulsa. The Freudian part of it was obvious, of course, but there was also something about

A cabaret scene from *Splendor in the Grass*

their pulling the wealth out of the ground and leaving the ground that reminded me of strip-mining.

Although it's unobtrusive, I did much more work on the scenery and costume in this picture than I ever did before – much more carefully. I had two sets repainted after they were finished; I wanted the actors to stand out from them, not be lost in them. I designed Barbara's dress for the party. I'm no designer, but I knew just what I wanted. I pinned it on her and cut it off at the bottom. I was very careful about all the clothes in this picture, about getting not only a feeling of the period but a feeling of drama. I didn't want it to look like a museum but as if they lived in the clothes. I think the black and red in the night-club was the art director's idea. The New Year's Eve scene was great. I had to know what the music was in order to shoot the scene a certain way. I had to have an idea of the music because I left pauses for it.

I wanted to make that ball scene in the colour of a bath-tub or like champagne – I had a lot of pastels all through it. The fight in the dark is wonderful. When I was a boy, at Williams College, there were a lot of fights in parking lots; the boys would come back later with their faces bloody, but arm in arm, that kind of thing. Of course, that's where it all comes from, Williams College! I was a waiter there – I was a waiter at that party, where Ginny danced – one of the waiters, one of the 'niggers'. There were also a lot of gang rapes in Kansas that Bill knew about. In a way it's similar to the South, that is, there's an appearance of courtesy, chivalry, hospitality, gifts, and drinks – but underneath it there's this terrific violence.

*It's also about the masks people wear.*

I found that myself on Broadway. Then I found that a lot of my friends who present themselves as models of rectitude, morality, and everything else were really prigs and full of hatred, full of animosity. Without blaming them, I said: Well, they do use both faces, many people have two faces. Ace Stamper is that way: he has to keep up a mask of masculinity and it is a terrible burden for a man; he can't get an erection at all times, he can't be powerful at all times, he's got to have the right to be weak and human and need help. And maybe he has strength at certain moments. It's the same with a woman – a woman can't be understanding and loving at all times. She might hate you most of the time – or half the time. Ace Stamper 'puts on the Hemingway act'. He's happy only in the company of men, he hasn't any use for women or understanding of them. He would say: 'How do you deal with a woman? What do they want?'

As for Bud, you want to know the truth? I think he is sort of scared of her, after she comes out of the institution. She is too complicated for him. I think he felt: 'I've got a nice wife, she doesn't make any demands on me, we help each other, we have the same aspirations, I'm comfortable here, what the hell do I need more trouble for? What do I need romance for? It's bullshit!' He's happy that way. I think he realises: this is what I want. The American notion, that love is the solution of all life's problems, is only true for an inhibited society. Even if you get the right woman you still have the same problems: you have to solve them within yourself.

# 9: Ego: *America America* (1964), *The Arrangement* (1969)

*When did you first go back to Asia Minor?*

When I was twelve we went to Turkey. It was 1921, right before the catastrophe of Smyrna. My father went on a business trip, and he took my mother and me. I met my relatives. But I don't remember that trip too vividly. Then I didn't go back for many, many years. It was 1956 or 1957 and I was already thinking about making a film about my uncle, and how he got to America. I went far into the interior for the first time, to the village in the heart of Asia Minor where my father was born. It was a tremendous experience, one I've never forgotten. In this community of Kayseri and in Germeer, where my mother's father was born, there were still houses that were empty, all broken down, where the Greeks used to live. The Turks, the old ones, remembered the Greeks with affection. The whole history of the relationship was bloody, murderous, but these people remembered the others with affection. It started my desire to write.

*America America* is the conclusion of your enquiry about your roots and the roots of America.

The longest life any story ever had in my mind was from the time I was five and my grandmother told me stories about the massacres of Asia Minor, to the time when I was fifty-five, when I finally did *America America*. I'd always wanted to tell how my family came here. I started to tell a story about someone else – Stavros – and gradually tried to turn it into a story about myself. And it becomes more and more like myself. I play out the same struggles I've always had: the struggle to find my own dignity, my own self, the struggle to impress other people, the struggle to be rich, and the struggle to remain honest. I always oppose money and purity; I always think, if a person is rich he must be a bastard. Maybe that's from my communist days, maybe it's religious.

*America America* was close to me on a lot of things; it came from my own life. I slowly, on tiptoe, get closer and closer to really saying: this is about me. It's both an ending and a beginning. It's the first screenplay I wrote by myself; and I was determined, now, to write my own movies, completely. To my surprise, I got very good reactions to the screenplay from all my friends. But every motion picture company turned it down and Warner Brothers first.

Finally we got it financed by Ray Stark. We got the crew and I cast it and we were in the Istanbul Hilton when I got a telephone call from my lawyer, William Fitelson, saying: 'Ray Stark has backed out.' I said: 'How can he back out now? We're here, with a crew, they're running up bills in the bar, drinking daiquiris, what am I going to do?' He said: 'Ray Stark tells you to sue him! Go ahead, but he's not going to make the picture.' He had given the script to some friends to read and they advised him against it. We were getting ready to shoot in a couple of days, unpacking our equipment, I had been meeting with the Turkish censors, with every department in the Government, and we had no money! I had about 500 dollars in travellers' cheques, and the costume designer had 200 dollars cash and we put some money together to pay for that day's bills. Fitelson went with his hat in his hand, on his knees, to Warner Brothers and said: 'Please – my friend, your friend Kazan, who made so much money for you, is in difficulties. Please. I know you don't like the picture, nobody likes it, I'll admit, but do him a good turn. Back this goddamn picture!' Against their better judgment, they backed the picture; and of course their opinion was right. They lost a million and a half dollars on it! That's the way it started. We had nothing but adventures on that picture.

I had a lot of notes, but I wrote the screenplay in one burst, over four months, a few pages a day. I think it was 1961. *Hamal* was the first name of the screenplay, the second *The Anatolian Smile*, and the third *America America*.

*It's about your uncle, Joe Kazan.*

Stavros (Stathis Giallelis) carries his dead Armenian friend from the church burned by Turks

The basic stories in that picture are true. For instance, all the family's wealth was put on a donkey; the donkey was turned over to my uncle. He was to drive it to Constantinople, to a relative. He lost the money on the way. No one knows exactly how. He met a bandit, he said. He arrived there penniless. He swept the floors of rug stores, just like my character. He resented it. He worked his way up by all kinds of conniving. He reached America, he told me, by winning the favours of a married woman who gave him the fare (whether he went on the same boat or not, no one knows). Many people wanted their daughters to marry him, because he looked like he was going to be successful, and he was a handsome young man. Those were his boasts. The essential story is true – except for the Hamal incident. He would never have done that. The shoeshine boy is not true of my uncle; though at that time they were bringing over a lot of Greeks to be shoeshine boys and making them work for nothing for two years. Of course I read all that, I spoke to Greeks who'd come over that way.

I knew Joe Kazan intimately. I did all kinds of things with him. He used to take me to the races; he used to give me 100 dollars at Christmas. He was very, very wealthy at one time; he had a Rolls Royce, the first one I ever saw. He used to drive me around. I went to his apartment: he had a girl-friend, he had a gym in his apartment. He lived in the Ritz Towers Hotel. He was several times a million-aire. He gave presents, he was generous, he was a bastard. Then I went to college and I didn't see him for a while; and when I came back three or four years later he was absolutely broke. He was like a madman. He was coming to my father's office and yelling at him: 'Loan me some money, give me some money!' He really went from the bottom to the top to the bottom. That curve is what I'm going to write about in my next book. That's the whole story of this insane social system that we have in America. In many ways I admire him. He was a man who had a good time. My father was a very cautious man, very careful, very I-know-nothing, self-effacing and masked. This fellow was tricky, but in a good-natured way. He said: 'All right, I'm a crook, now let's do business.'

My uncle enjoyed being an American capitalist, a wheeler-dealer, for him it was civilisation. He had no guilt about it, he had no morals, he didn't go to church. He wrote three books, *60 Minutes Experience*, *Life of Kazanova*, *My Life at the Race-Track*, when he didn't have a quarter. He had to go to his old friends and embarrass them to get money to publish the books. They're about his philosophy – terrible stuff! A recurrent theme: 'Don't trust any woman.' His mistress had money when he was broke, and she wouldn't give him any. He was a very colourful, real character. You couldn't help liking him. He played the races every day and he never slept in a bed. He used to sleep on a sofa. When he went to Europe on the *Ile de France* or the *Aquitania* he had the sofa taken on the boat and then from the boat to the hotel in Paris.

I have photographs of him, and he changed completely. When he was a young man of twenty-two to twenty-three and first came to this country, he looked very upright, very erect; and he was. He was the head of the family. He took his responsibilities very seriously. He brought all his family here, even the brothers he didn't like, his half-brothers, his stepmother – I don't know how fond he was of her. And one by one they all turned against him. The last part of his life was a whole feeling of 'You can't trust anybody, you mustn't turn your back to anybody.' But he didn't say that in a mean way – he laughed about it. He was a cynic rather than a misanthrope.

At the end, Stavros is beginning to be a cynic. The last thing I show Stavros doing in *America America* is, he gets a quarter tip, throws it up in the air and catches it. You feel he understands what America is. In order to get to America, you have to be tough, you have to go for the money, you have to protect yourself. If your back is to the wall you have to use any means to protect your life. And it's either him or me in capitalism, right? Capitalism is a jungle, right? And it's either he dies or I die, in the jungle, right? That's actually what he felt. That was the lesson of life, to him. There are good people, you trust them, they're weak, they die, only the tough survive. You have to win the dogfight, that's all. I think the audience sees a man shaped into a monster by the pressures of his time. I always thought he should end up a monster, a tough little New York kid. Remorse dies – in this man, anyway. You feel it for a while, and then ... It hasn't died in me, but in this man it dies.

*The film is shaped not only by your memories but by your work. Mrs Kebabian is like a Tennessee Williams character.*

Mrs Kebabian is like a second cousin I have, who really had culture, played the piano, could sing, read, and she was in the hands of a man who did absolutely nothing but do business all day. And my mother's like that: my mother reads books – and my father never read a book in his life. They were all captives of men as vulgar, uncultured, and indifferent to refinement as you can imagine. In their leisure, they play cards – and cards are business in the form of a game. She is like a Williams character; but she's also very typical of the woman in that society.

*You reconcile documentary and drama.*

Yes, I wanted this documentary style. Not romantic. The picture of the steerage in the boat is terrific. The arrival on Ellis Island is the best shot I ever made in my life – those people on Ellis Island. Then I did the corniest thing of all – when Stavros arrives to America he gets on his knees and kisses the ground. It's as corny as you can get. Everybody said to me: 'For Chrissake, don't put that in the picture, they'll laugh at you, it'll be a joke!' I said: 'That's what they did.' My uncle did it. He got down on his knees and kissed the ground. That's

Stavros and Hohanness (Gregory Rozakis) on the boat to America

what America meant. And another thing I was saying to Americans in the picture: look what people gave up, what they put themselves through, to come to this country – it's your responsibility to make it worth their sacrifice.

*Adultery plays an important part in your films.*

It was on my mind. It's one of my environments. I was brought up to believe, when I was a boy, that adultery was a sin. As soon as I became an adult, my education said, that's ridiculous, it depends on the situation, what's behind it. But still somewhere in me, I still think of it as reprehensible, that it's wrong. It's as though something bad is going to happen to the person doing it. I don't believe it in my mind, but I think I'm ambivalent as a person. I'm both very moral and very unrestrained. I don't think anything is a sin, abstractly. It depends on whom you hurt and how much. Sometimes it's necessary. I think hurting other people is bad, but I don't think you can go through life without hurting other people. All you can do is hurt them as little as you can, or not hurt them if you can possibly help it. But I was brought up, actually, to think sex was a sin.

*The Armenian represents nationalism, Garabet socialist struggle, Hohanness the Christian ideal. All three fail. Does this imply that anything beyond a personal struggle is doomed to fail?*

That's a possible interpretation. But what the film is obviously dealing with is a particular situation at a particular time in a particular milieu. I did mean to say that at that time, there was no outlet for the feeling of anger and rebellion and dislocation in a young man through the means of nationalism; this revolt was crushed immediately, the nationalists being completely outnumbered, terrorised, slaughtered on suspicion. Education was kept from them. The authorities saw to it that they only got to the eighth grade. Nor was there any outlet through anarchism – Garabet represents anarchism, not socialism – propaganda through deeds, protests, bombing. There were bombings in the streets of Istanbul, but very little programme. It was also squashed without mercy, it had no chance, it had no organisation. The young man in the film sees that. And Christianity, while it preserved certain elements of nationalism and of the language, was at the same time a reactionary force which said to people: 'Stay out of social struggle. Stay quiet. Stay inside yourself. Come into church, it is safe there.' I show in the film that the church is not safe, it's burned down, and as the people run out they're shot down.

Stavros knows that if he stays with Thomna he'll always be a minority person, and frightened. Her family gives him everything in the world. That's why I made them flatter him so much, be that generous with him: I made it as hard as possible for him to go away. But he did because he had his family waiting.

When these immigrants arrived in America, they found themselves in a society that was also not welcoming, but where everybody *could* get along through his wits. They came to a very simple philosophy, which was: if you had a dollar, you were safe, you had status and pleasure, through the accumulation of money. Maybe I should have made it clearer, saying *they* felt that way but *I* don't. I did try to locate it in that society, and dramatise the repressive forces as being so terrible, so complete, and so final that Stavros had no choice. We're living on a very thin skin of civilisation.

*Maybe it has to do with your own disillusionment with nationalism, socialism, Christianity.*

One is always dealing with symbols. You're saying something, not just telling a story; you are in some way or other conveying a meaning. Everything they learned in church meant: 'Keep your eyes to the ground when you walk the streets where the Turks are.' You survived through your religion. By the time I got to be a young man, I didn't believe that. I thought that religion was a menace, dangerous and harmful. I believe that socialism will win in the world – maybe not fast enough in every way, but it is going that way. Imperialist capitalism is a preposterous thing. As for nationalism, I'm for it some times and not others. It depends who's dealing in nationalism. And when. Finally I'm against it.

*Many objects in the film are pregnant with meaning.*

There are a lot of them in this picture: the grandmother's necklace, the knife that he always carries, the fez and the straw hat, and the shoes which mean a lot to me because I've seen a lot of poverty in my life. All poor people have a thing about shoes.

*How did you cast the film?*

Well, in the first place, they're all unknown, you've never seen them before, which is a great help, because they're not 'actors'. In the second place, I chose people who were Jews or Greeks. Rozakis and Antonio are Greeks, Linda Marsh, Paul Mann and Harry Davis are Jews. All of them know oppression, they all have uncles from the 'Old World' and have an affectionate relationship towards their forbears. I cast Stathis Giallelis from what he told me about his youth in Greece. His father was a communist and he was captured by the Right and beaten around the kidneys. He began to bleed internally and it was a very slow and painful death. Giallelis held him in his arms as he died. At the age of fifteen he had to support his family and to help his three sisters and his younger brother. What I saw right away in Stathis was a little man, a boy with the duties of a man. He was determined, hateful, longing, and sweet and cruel. His face had all this because he had been through them all. I encouraged him and finally he came by himself to America. Considering that he had never acted before on the screen or on the stage Stathis did a magnificent job. I can't think of anyone else who could have played that role better. He was it.

The Ellis Island scene was shot in an old Greek customs-house. These people were refugees, from the other side of the Iron Curtain. There were great camps in the north of Greece where the people who ran across the border from Roumania, Albania and Bulgaria were put. We sent some trucks up there and got them and brought them back. They looked like the real thing, they had that rough skin that no professional extras have. If I had shot it in America, in Hollywood, it would've been dead. But those people's faces . . . Some brought their own costumes. I think that's the best production, from the point of view of costumes and scenery, that I ever did. It looks like a film made fifty years ago, as well as a film made now.

*Haskell Wexler, the cameraman, had made documentary films.*

Wexler was the only cameraman I have ever worked with whom I didn't like personally. I wanted to hit him a few times, but, at the same time, I admired him. He was as good a man with hand-held as I'd ever seen. He's almost like a human crane. He can start on his feet with a hand-held camera, and go down as someone falls, go right down to him, smooth and easy – he's marvellous with it. He did all his own hand-held work.

*The sound-track is particularly precise.*

Before, I was very much at fault about sound, but in the last years I've become terribly aware of it. In this picture, wherever I went, when I heard a sound I liked, I told the sound man to get it, so he could put it in the back of some scene. Somewhere there was a bird singing; I quietened everyone down so he could record it. It only cost two minutes, and I had a unique track. I wish I'd been more attuned to that in *Wild River*; I could have got sounds of people walking through the corn, I could have got sounds of the water flowing by – I missed a lot, and I shouldn't have, because I worked in radio a lot when I was a young actor.

*You had some problems with the Turkish censorship.*

Every time somebody from their government came to meet me to talk about arrangements, he always came into my hotel room, looked around, and said: 'Come on out.' I had a little balcony, and we always discussed there. The room was bugged.

I was going to stay three weeks in Turkey and we stayed only four days. On the fifth day it got impossible. We had a censor on the set with us, and he was a terrified bureaucrat. In one shot the camera panned and went into some garbage heaped at the side. I used to hold his head so he couldn't turn it. Afterwards he objected. 'For God's sake don't do that. I'm sympathetic to you personally, but they're going to kill me!' That afternoon, the fifth afternoon, I had some scenes where we show some Turks bargaining, waving their hands a little vulgarly. All of a sudden a man in a grey suit runs out of the crowd and yells at the censor: 'Why do you let him do that?' They had the secret police watching the censor. They had a terrible fight, and the censor disappeared; I never saw him again. The secret police told me: 'You can't do that! You make fools of the Turks!' So I said: 'Wrap it up, we're going to Greece.' We hid the reels of film we had exposed in 'unexposed' boxes, and I shot the rest of the film in Athens.

*Each 'chapter' of the film has its own movement.*

That's where Hadjidakis helped me; he put things together through music. He characterised each episode with a different kind of music and a different rhythm. I don't think I succeeded as well as I might have but I wanted every episode to have a different feeling. I think there's one episode too many, but I don't know which one. I played with tempo for the first time. When a tempo is uniform it begins to seem slow. When the rhythm is the same it becomes monotonous even in fast-moving things. It took me a long time to learn it, but if you alternate a slow scene and a fast one, the fast scene seems faster, and the slow scene seems deeper. In *America America* I alternated violence and tenderness. The idea of the Paul Mann scene was to make him wistful, and harden him at the same time – to make him feel that he was losing his daughter. I tried to do that sequence as tenderly as I could. All through the film I alternated rhythms. I also treated Stavros as several different characters under the pressure of the events he goes through. I made the changes, the stages of his development more abrupt and more startling. At the beginning, he's a dutiful boy; on the road, when he gets robbed, he's a yokel; when he gets to town and works on the docks, he's hard-fisted, like an animal almost, a dog, a cur; then, when he's in the house, he's like a Romeo!

I exaggerated so you would feel the change and, as a result, feel the movement of the time more.

I cut the 'bridges', the things that lead you from one shot to another, and I made abrupt transitions. I did it on purpose, to surprise the audience. It also makes for drama, because you wonder how he got there. Where did he get his clothes, when he went courting? I don't explain it, whereas I did in the book.

*How did you come to write your first novel,* The Arrangement*?*

Well, of course, my first language is not English; and I never studied writing. I'm not much of a stylist, but I have had a lot happen to me in my life, and I'm not embarrassed to say things, so I'm a good story-teller, I think. I open myself up; a writer is a man who is in touch with himself. When I was in college I didn't do any writing at all, except trying to write poetry, secretly. At Yale, I tried to write plays. They were no good, but I kept trying. To me, writers were the élite. They were the people that I, as a director and an actor, served.

Sometimes life forces you into things and this is how I really became a writer. I had gone into Lincoln Center in 1963 for personal and not for artistic reasons. It's not in my nature to go to the same place every day to be tied to it. I'm for repertory theatres, but I couldn't run one. So when my wife died in 1963, I decided to get out of it as fast as I could. Also, I had no more interest in the Actors' Studio. Strasberg was running it happily, and I could go there whenever I wanted to experiment or find actors. And something about the nature of my relationship with my first wife had made it hard for me to write. Suddenly, with her death, I felt I was going to write a book. So I went to my partner at Lincoln Center, Bob Whitehead, and told him: 'I'm never going to do any more plays – I'm through.' This was my chance to become a writer; if I meant it, my chance was now. So I went to France, took a room in a hotel on the Left Bank, and started to write what I remembered of my life. Gradually, over a period of months, this book became *The Arrangement*.

I wrote about my mother, my father, my youth, elements in my own life. What helped me most was my psychoanalysis, because I'd been psychoanalysed into articulation, into wishing to speak. It was the most helpful thing that ever happened; the whole thing of just *talking*. Slowly, after about three months, it began to be a story. Then I wrote the book.

If you are writing a long novel in which you express yourself fully, you can't do anything else because the experience is so complete. I left a lot of my friends, I broke off, not in a hostile way, I became a lone creature, which is the fate of a creator. When I finished the novel, it was twice as long as it is now. My editor Sol Stein and I cut about 200,000 words out of it. I never expected it to be a success; it was a total, complete surprise to me that anybody was interested in it. It was No. 1 for thirty-seven weeks. It got many bad notices and some good ones, but that didn't make any difference. I realised I had spoken something that people had themselves experienced: this book excited empathy. It was my final declaration of independence.

*The hero is three men in the book: Evangeli, the son of immigrants, Eddie Anderson, the publicist, and Evans Arness, the writer. In the movie the writer is more or less discarded.*

That's absolutely true, and I think it's regrettable. I don't blame Kirk Douglas for this, I blame only myself; but Kirk is not acceptable, really, as a writer, where Brando would have been. Kirk is perfect as a publicist – I don't think you could get anyone better on the aggressive side. He's a complete salesman: his product is Kirk Douglas, he sells it. My main problem was that there was too much material for a two-hour picture. I think *The Arrangement* should have been longer. Once I had it twenty minutes longer, and something in me found it too 'long'. I was affected by the same goddamn thing the audience was affected by – the idea there should be a standard length. It's preposterous. But now I'm going to make films their own length.

I like this picture, but I think I could have done much better. I made a terrible mistake – accepting an offer of a million dollars. It turned out less actually – but still it was a substantial sum of money. I should have made that picture with a smaller crew around New York; I should have borrowed an advertising office somewhere and got unknown actors. It would have been a hundred times better. I could have had the hero just walk around New York City and his voice reading parts from the book; then I would have had some of his reflective side, moments of rest instead of the drive. I think you would have believed that side of him more if the advertising agency hadn't been so glamorous, so insistent.

I've always been more at home in real locations than in Hollywood, because I think I've done better work that way. I can see why *Citizen Kane* could only have been made in a studio, the way Orson Welles thought of it. There are other directors, like Joe Mankiewicz who's really a superb director of high comedy and satire, who are much more at home in studios, dealing with highly charged personalities, stars. And of course musicals are, on the whole, better in studios. There should be something artificial (in the good sense) about their *mise en scène* and costumes.

*The film is different from the book in the use of flashbacks.*

The flashbacks made Eddie behave differently. Arthur Miller also did that in *Death of a Salesman*. One thing I admired about that play was that, because of what was shown in the flashbacks, the behaviour of the central character was different when it came back to the present. The flashback wasn't just generally descriptive, but the presence of the memory affected the behaviour of the leading character. Without the flashbacks, I couldn't have got the mother/father material in, which was absolutely necessary: the mother encouraged him to become an artist and to have faith in himself. The father taught him the other orientation: he acted tough. When he goes to the bank, he wants to impress the bank employees.

What is better in the film is the ending: the funeral with the thruways all around and going by. This man who came over here, went through all this misery and raised a family, died right in the middle of a traffic jam! And the way the family's gathered there, all the opposing elements, who don't look at each other, and then separate ... The end of the book, on the contrary, is a little on the level of soap-opera. Being in Los Angeles, you're aware of this terrible traffic, these thruways – the trucks do pile up behind you, and it does seem as if they're going to run over you. One day I saw this graveyard in the middle of this thruway and I thought, that's the end of the film.

*Why did you start it with the accident?*

I thought it created the basis for a psychological mystery story. Why did he kill himself? I should have done that in the book too. By the time you get to it in the book, you know the reasons pretty well. As far as the accident itself is concerned, the book is better; it happens almost in spite of Eddie, he does not understand it, whereas in the film you feel he does it on purpose, which I think was wrong. He jerks the wheel around; it would be better if the wheel slowly turns, he's thinking of something else and suddenly has an accident.

I think Gwen is better in the film than in the book. There's less of her, but what is there is more human, not so much an imagined figure. And Deborah Kerr is better than Florence in the book. Her figure is softer, whereas her character in the book is caricatured. It's very confusing to do both film and book. I'm not sure I'll ever do it again.

*Both this film and* America America *are criticisms of the 'success story'.*

All the characters are conditioned by the society they live in. Florence is a frightened woman in the sense that she has never lived without money. Gloria has a failure for a husband, so she gets on his back and rides him like a horse, and tries to make him become 'a man', more aggressive, not so soft. That's another side of the same thing. Eddie has always made a good living for Florence. The other dame feels, what did I marry this schmuck for? He's not unfaithful to me constantly, like *her* husband, but he never brings me any money in. That's what *she* is.

Eddie and Gwen don't have much in common. What she means to him hasn't a lot to do with sex, but she is a person who isn't other-directed. She's inner-directed, she makes her own evaluation of things, and I think that's what leads him to her. She's honest, that's what gets him. And he finds that his wife, who's puritanical, who was brought up with perfect manners, is dishonest. Also, she's against everything he believes in, morally. She's a moral villain, a moral criminal. There's always an element of change in my films. I understand he has to leave and hurt his wife, and I understand that Gwen is going to hurt him some day. I try to foreshadow it. I feel *necessity* very strongly, the dialectic of progress through two forces hitting each other.

*Is the film an answer to* America America? *Do you criticise America because it did not turn out to be what the immigrants expected?*

Yes. And I think there's an element of love in it. The only disappointment that's painful is with someone you love and for whom you had

Gwen (Faye Dunaway) and Eddie (Kirk Douglas) in *The Arrangement*

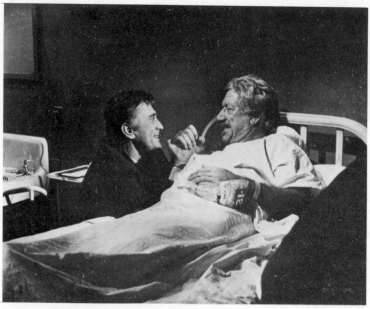

*The Arrangement*: Eddie visits his father (Richard Boone) in hospital

hopes. In this society, there are thousands and thousands of people who earn their living doing something, which they not only detest but know is killing them. They sell their lives to make a living. A lot of these men have a secret hope that some day they'll write something, or do something they respect. There are all kinds of secret, forlorn, incapable artists in this society. I worked in an office when I was a kid, during the summer, and I never forgot going down into the subway, and the stench of the perspiring people, the stale smell, and the terrible faces, the resentful faces, the tension.

Eddie Anderson, in *The Arrangement*, gave up his soul just as his uncle Stavros did. The story of *The Arrangement* is how he gets it back. The end of the film is hopeful. It's a happy ending, even though it's painful. You have to pay for happiness. He sacrifices a lot: a home, a decent wife, money, security; and he doesn't know where he's at the end. But he's more stable within himself. When he stands by the grave, I try to show that he has become a man. But I

160

think if I had had Brando, that scene would be better, although Kirk was good in the picture so many times. If it had been Brando, you would have felt something shining in him. What Kirk had was strength. But there should also have been something weak, uncertain still. With Kirk I lost certain things, with Brando I might have lost others. It wasn't a matter of understanding, Kirk has an excellent mind. It's a matter of character and artistic habits.

*Where did you get the idea of the wild dogs and the giraffes on television?*

That's stuff my friend Hume Cronyn shot in Africa. I've never seen anything that better describes the way the critics, or business people tear somebody up if he shows any sign of weakness ... It's the equivalent of what's written in the book about fish under water in the Bahama Islands; on the outside of the herds of fish are a few barracuda, and they just swim along watching, as if they were looking after them, tenderly. Then suddenly, there's a fish that wavers a little bit, a little uncertainty that no one else sees, except the barracuda, and, CRUNCH! he's gone.

*How did you work on the colours with Surtees? What kind of effect did you want?*

Well, the colours came out a little brighter than I wanted them. What I asked Surtees to get was a black and white effect in colour. There's nothing new about that! But I found out in this film that I liked the rushes better than the final print. By the time the lab got through improving my print, it didn't look right. The more prints they put out, the worse it looked. I've found out since that the only way to get the colour greyed down is to fog the negative, to expose it a little bit. The Technicolor laboratories were devised to create candy – another kind of entertainment for people. '*Oh, how colourful! Look at that colour!*' It's *colourful*. And it's a disaster. I liked the colour in *Splendor in the Grass*, I thought that was very appropriate, those gaudy colours, but not in *The Arrangement*, except in the scenes in the advertising world because *it is* that world.

Let me say this: though it has defects, *The Arrangement* is a damn unusual picture. It is about a 'successful' American; it deals with social and psychoanalytical criticism and has to do with the past, the worth, and the nature of America. I feel that today film-makers who make films that have social significance, instead of doing what I hope I've tried to – which is making the films exactly about contemporary issues – make metaphors. They say: 'It's a Western but it's really about Vietnam' or 'It's a gangster story but it's really about the difficulty of speaking the truth in America', etc. In other words, they make substitute pictures. I've often wondered why no one of the Hollywood Ten has ever written a film or a novel about their experience. I think a work telling the outrages of the McCarthy period, as seen by people who suffered very terribly by it, would have been welcomed. I mean a really strong book (those men are all novelists, you know), broad in scope and deep in its feelings, because they certainly felt it deeply. It was a bad experience for them, and I've often wondered why they didn't speak directly about it. I think the answer to that question – why did we as a generation get into the habit of making so many metaphors? – is that there was a period at the end of the thirties and in the forties where the whole socio-political technique of film-makers was 'How much can we get away with, how much can we *say*?' without the Jack Warners or Louis B. Mayers knowing that we were 'saying' something that was Left. How much can we fool them by getting some little morsel of social significance into a film that was not about that at all. And that became a habit of mind, in all these people – a way of thinking and a way of working. Of all of us, myself included. It was one thing I had to confront and change.

# 10: Them: *The Visitors* (1971), *The Assassins* (1971)

In *The Visitors* there is a central creative effort to make the rapists, the American soldiers who have become brutalised, very much the sons of America, people with genuine longings for love and the more tender and lasting things in life. What I particularly like is moments like the one when the father and the young stranger lie on the sofa and fall asleep arm in arm. The fact that the father likes the boy so much, that the boy has such tenderness when he says 'She's a good-looking girl' ... You feel that it's his dream to have a wife and a home like that, that he doesn't just come there for revenge and carry it out, that his own tender feelings are a complicating factor. In a sense, that's exactly what America is. These boys did do those brutal things over there; there's no doubt that Calley and Medina and those fellows were brutalised. But to just call them monsters is to avoid the problem. Whenever you point and say: 'That fellow is a villain,' you can hold the whole issue at arms' length and say: 'Oh, that's those bad boys, those psychos, it's not *me*.' What we tried to do was to depict those two characters so that the audience could not escape. There's no exit from that picture. That's why we built it up so slowly. You get to like the visitors, you see what they are, you recognise them; you see their interest in football, the all-American sport; and then all of a sudden they do a shocking thing, they kill that dog. After that again they behave in a familiar way, march like boys, play on the ice like boys, throw a football around, and they girl-watch, all classic American boy activities. Before you know it, you're back being sympathetic with them, right? They're 'nice guys'. The whole point of brutality in war is that the nicest people do it. The sweetest, the most lovable, the most affectionate people do it.

*How did you come to work in super 16mm?*

Well, Barbara helped me a lot, in the sense that the experience she had with *Wanda* was very influential. She introduced me to Proferes, her cameraman. I saw her shooting, I worked around the edges in *Wanda*. I was the second assistant director, handled the crowds in the bank scene, advised on lighting, moved some props around, and so on. I minded her children while she was doing it, helped her raise the money, worked a little bit on the script, and did odd jobs. It was a great lesson to me, that this whole thing about film production had been built up into a monster that is a detriment, not an asset. I decided to do with an even smaller crew. I had a camera crew of only three men. It was like a test, to see how simple, how relaxed a film production could be. I don't think there's anything technically inferior about this picture. And it was made for nothing. Also, when I wanted to make a scene over (we did many scenes over, in this picture, because we had new actors except the old man), there was no reason why I couldn't do it over right away, because it cost so little. So I had much more freedom as an artist, making *The Visitors* on 135,000 dollars, than I had making *The Arrangement* on 6,800,000 dollars, where there is only a million and a half maybe on the screen. The rest of it is unaccounted for, diverted to other uses.

This lesson will affect the rest of my life. I was thinking, how did Hollywood get to have such big crews? I think it has something to do with the fact that one of the problems, originally, was to photograph older women and older men so they looked younger; and also that they were selling glamour, superficial effects of kitsch beauty. Furthermore, it got to be a melon that everybody wanted a piece of, and so there were lots of people running around with knives out. During my first picture at Fox, I had a fellow who followed me around with a chair, and every time I stopped he'd put the chair under me! I don't sit down a great deal, but this man was always there with the chair, and he'd say to me: 'Let me get you something to drink.' It embarrassed me, he was a big, tall guy, a nice fellow, and I realised that this man was there, assigned, only to keep me in a state of flattery. But on *The Visitors* I carried the tripod, I arranged the properties, I shovelled snow when there was snow in the driveway, I moved the cars around – did the whole goddamn thing. It was like going back to the days when I made that documentary in Tennessee. It was a very cleansing experience. We didn't have many lights, but we didn't need them! I wasn't handicapped in any way.

It's also easier to do hand-held work with 16mm. I'd say about 80% of our shots were hand-held. You also need less light, and you can get it into corners where it's very hard to get a heavier camera. Super-16mm stock has about 30% more negative space, exposure space, so there'll only be a few spots where there's some graininess. I don't think graininess hurts pictures much, unless you have a Hollywood standard of wax-fruit beauty, where everything has to have a smooth skin.

*As in all your recent films, you have a mixture of social and psychoanalytical: the film has two levels, conscious and unconscious.*

I feel we all live on an edge. If we get a bit upset, if we have a few nights with no sleep, if a girl-friend leaves us, all of a sudden we're doing things we can't normally imagine doing. It's the same thing about the quiet scenery; the surface, when you first see it, is pleasant, complacent, pretty, but underneath it are these possibilities. In America this is more so than in other countries, because it's more in turmoil, more changing, more unsettled in its elements.

In the first half-hour of this picture, I try to suggest an ominous quality; but I try to do it much more lightly than I would have twenty years ago, when I'd have had symbolic and blacker things. *The Visitors*, though, is off the route where I was going, in the sense that it's not personal. And part of it is accidental. My son Chris has always wanted to make pictures; and one day we were talking and I suggested this idea to him: what happens after My Lai; suppose those boys come back to this country, what happens? That's all I said to him, just something I threw off. He went and wrote the script. I thought it was excellent. He said: 'Would you like to direct it?' and I said: 'Why don't you direct it?' But no, he wanted me to, and so I did it. To my eyes, it doesn't have many autobiographical elements. It's cooler, it's more an objective view of what I feel America is like.

*You confront the bad conscience of the young man about the Vietnam War and the attitude of the old man towards World War Two.*

That old man is so naïve! He doesn't know a thing. That psychology – we intervened, we're going to save Europe, we're going to make the world safe for democracy, really has something so arrogant about it,

combined with stupidity. What the hell, let's make our own country safe for democracy, since we still haven't got democracy in many respects here. That's what we tried to represent in that person.

The most interesting character in this film, to me, is the girl, because there's this terrifying ambivalence about her. On the one hand, she's living and sleeping with this man, but she won't marry him. There's something missing: her father is not in this boy. What she finds missing in the boy is the very thing she despises in her mind. She marches in the anti-war parades, but she misses in her lover the violence and strength that would have made him shoot that dog when it threatened her. She bullies the man, and at the same time she wishes he were stronger. And that's typical of this country.

In the same way, she dresses up for the visitor, puts a ribbon on, takes her sweater off, has a pink blouse on. She finds his sensitivity. That's why, when she lies on the sofa, she touches his coat, she feels almost motherly towards him, as though he needs someone. She's touched by him. Then the next minute, after they start to fight, she turns around and defends her husband again. It's a fascinating character. She sometimes looks very cruel, and very harsh; and other times she looks like a baby. The actresses I like (Barbara is one of them) are able to look both plain and lovely, good-looking and brutish, to be both cruel and sweet. This girl is just a beginner, but she has some of that quality.

As for the young man she's living with, he resents the father because he intuits how much of a hold he has on his daughter. There's something masochistic about him, no doubt about it. Still he's struggling against this masochism, because he keeps reading that paper, looking for a house, through the whole time of the film – but he never does anything, he's still there at the end. He should have just left, months ago.

*The fight in the dark is reminiscent of your other films.*

Yes, but I did it better here, partly because of the necessary economy in making the picture. The car is visible, behind it they're fighting, but you don't see them. Because of the lack of money, we couldn't light that field, but it's more telling than if I'd shown it all.

*There's a single flashback: the rape of the Vietnamese girl.*

I have to explain it backwards. The shot immediately following the

167

After the fight sequence in *The Visitors*: Chico Martinez and James Woods flashback is of Steve lying on the back of the old car they've driven up in. It's a close shot of his face, and you can read his face; he's really wonderful as an actor at that moment, he gives a marvellous internal performance. What I feel, what I hope the audience will too, is the fact that he remembers with regret what he did to that girl. He remembers it with a sense of pain. You cannot discard him or despise him: he's a sensitive boy. It goes back to Cal in *East of Eden*: he's the bad boy, but you look at him and say: evil and good are mixed. Now, in order to get that shot, it seemed to me that the flashback would have to be there, or else it wouldn't be motivated emotionally. The emotion is specifically directed, in the sense that, having raped another girl upstairs, he remembers that Vietnamese that he hurt. His guilt is motivated by the flashback.

*It is interesting that one of the veterans is Puerto Rican.*

Chris chose that. I don't think the Puerto Rican has really forgiven either, though he means it when he says he has. All through the picture, you see his resentment in glimpses. And then he gets friendly again. There's a certain thing that develops in minority people whether they like to admit it or not, and that the new blacks and the new Puerto Ricans have abandoned. In the majority of them in this country there's a sort of compliance, a sort of getting along with society, of pretending to be friendlier than they are. He has that smile, he gets along.

*Everything is related in the film.*

Chris has an integrated conceptual mind. He sees the world *totally*. He's very sharp, doesn't speak too readily or too easily, but relates everything in life to his central way of viewing things. There is a pattern of violence, in every particular – including the girl's violence over her boy-friend – even to the baby when she's down playing with his penis.

*Why did you shoot it in winter?*

I like the snow. It boxed the people in the house; they couldn't get away from each other. What you feel here is New England: Connecticut, Vermont, Massachusetts, Maine. Life opens up in the spring, you're free in the summer, it begins to close in in the fall, and in the winter you're trapped inside the cold, you can't go out. In

Maine, the barns are connected with the house, and the wood and the coal they burn in the fireplace is indoors, so you don't have to go outdoors at all. That was one of the feelings I tried to get.

*In the scene where they dance you extend the feeling of time passing.*

When he takes her arm and puts it on his shoulder and she just stands there waiting ... and then they begin to dance, and her hand moves up a little bit – I think that's the most economical sex scene I ever did in my life. Ten years ago I would have done much more, but I held myself back – I guess I'm getting old! I tried to do it with the least means possible.

The boy is terrific: he could be a star. That's his first picture and he's never acted in a play. He was trying to get into the Actors' Studio; they didn't accept him. Now they have. He was a typical sort of hippie; he only began to look right when we cut his hair. We tried to cast them very young, very childish, very innocent.

*Details of ordinary life, like the meat, take on symbolic overtones.*

Both Chris and I are very aware of it. What *is* a symbol, anyway? It's something that has a double meaning, a super-meaning, without losing its first simple meaning. I don't believe in it unless it has a perfectly well-grounded base realistically. Then it's not forced, not mannered, it's just the way people are. When I show it to you, you will see the other meanings. But you could pass it by in life and never see it. A good symbol is even capable of opposite meanings. Take the dog. That's clearly, to the people in the film, a symbol of menace, of danger, of death, I try to introduce it, therefore, in such a way that it's a symbol of life – running across the ice, jumping around – and it's terrible when they kill him, right? You're not sure exactly what it means. It stirs your mind.

As for the meat during the dinner, it is always put down in a different way. I don't think about it, but I do it by second nature. When Steve Railsback is looking up at Jim Woods scornfully, Pat McVey is carving his meat; Woods doesn't want to fight, but when McVey puts the meat on the plate he just flops it on, and instead of passing it directly to Bill, he passes it to Railsback, who passes it to the Puerto Rican, and the Puerto Rican looks at it and smiles, then hands it to him. You can't smell burnt meat in a film, you can't even see it clearly, but by the way they handle the meat, you can feel that it's the outside piece, the one real he-men don't like.

Another ridiculous example of this symbolism: the old man runs to the house and says: 'I knew there were Jerries in there,' and then he pulls out an imaginary grenade pin, opens the door of his house, throws the 'grenade', and says: 'Boom!' At that moment you see the soldiers, and they're looking at each other as if to say: 'This man is ridiculous.' That's a comedy incident, but it's also symbolic of the enormous changes between that war and this war. The house he blows up is his own house, so you feel it should be blown up, that it's finished. And the way the men look at each other, you feel they wouldn't care if he did blow the goddamn thing up – it means nothing to them. That's the difference between these two wars. This man is proud of his part in the other war, and these two kids are ashamed, embarrassed by their part in this war. They never even speak about it. They watch it like strangers.

*For* The Visitors, *there are no camera directions in the script.*

Well, I laugh at those things, you know; they're for college courses, for seminars. No director pays attention to them. I think professional scriptwriters put them in to impress the men who are paying their salaries. It means absolutely nothing. I just told Chris, write where it happens, try to describe the conditions under which it happens, and that's all – don't play around with long shot or dolly shot or 'the camera moves in'. I'll tell the crew – the best time to tell them is the night before if there's anything special I need – if I have a travelling shot or a crane shot (which I never do), so they can lay it out. I read the script over rather carefully the morning I start shooting and then I put it away, because if you start looking at the book to see if the actors say the words right, you're not watching the real thing happening, which is the total performance. So I just walk around and don't carry anything. I've done that since *Panic in the Streets*. It's the way they used to make Westerns, you know, by set-ups, not by dialogue.

*How did you cast the non-professionals?*

The first one I cast was the old man, because I knew him from the Actors' Studio. He has played in a lot of TV shows and some films. I think that part is not as well written as the others; it is unilinear and

Camaraderie: Patrick McVey with Steve Railsback in *The Visitors*

most of the time his actions are predictable. But you cannot blame
the actor. The girl was in Jay Leyda's class at Yale where I made a
speech once. She had eyeglasses on, and I was very struck by
something in her face. She looked very plain, but I thought she had
an inner beauty. As for Railsback, somebody had described him to
me, and I called up Texas, where he'd gone for a vacation with his
father, and I said: 'When you come back to New York, see me.' As
soon as I saw him, I liked him. But I did many improvisations with
him to try him out. The other boy, Bill, just walked into my office
and I liked him immediately. Because the film was inexpensive, I
could sometimes rehearse in the mornings much longer. When they
start working with me in the morning, they never have any leisure,
and if they get tired in the afternoon, I let them sleep for twenty
minutes or so. But I'm always rehearsing. Even when they're sitting
quietly, I go up to them and start talking to them about the next
scene. The pressure and the atmosphere of work are continuous. So
they get exhausted by the end of the day – that sonofabitch director

has never let them alone! Even if they're sitting and eating: 'Well, maybe I'll have you eat like that in the scene,' or if they're sleeping, 'Maybe I'll have you sleep in the back of the set.' The rehearsals are partly formal rehearsals, but partly just walking around together, talking.

There is no division, really, between life and acting. In other words, as an actor you try to live the part; and you try to make the tastes of the character your tastes; and strange things happen between the actors during the shooting of a film, which are extensions of the characters' lives. You can say that the director is meddling in other people's lives; he helps things to take place. These people were enjoying the snow and cold or being terrorised by it. I kept telling the Puerto Rican guy: 'Look out, your feet are getting wet, it's cold out here,' and he got so that every time he went out he felt the cold. He was wearing these shoes with very thin soles that were always wetting through. And that was a very good thing. You see how he walks, he looks like a city boy in the country.

*As a writer do you find any progression between* The Arrangement *and* The Assassins?

I have improved as a writer in *The Assassins*. I still don't think I'm much of a stylist. My style is rather unvaried, it hasn't many graces, more a series of direct statements that say what I've observed and felt. So that perhaps the feeling and the true, precise nature of the observation make up for the lack of literary gloss. I try to improve; but when I read a really good writer – Faulkner or Mailer – I feel I'm not a stylist and never will be.

*The Assassins* is much more direct and more objective than *The Arrangement*. I did it partly on purpose, because of the effects of the counter-culture on me. The young people were the first ones to react violently against this war, react more purely and more deeply than older people did. They are spiritually seeking a different kind of life, rejecting the middle-class, typically American one. The book is about the various kinds of assassination that are going on in this country: character-assassination, actual assassination, the frustrations of young people as they face the way authority is manipulated and put down.

I'm very present in the book; but when you read it, you say: 'Oh yes, I read that in the papers,' 'Oh yes, I saw this in films,' and so on.

And when it's all together you'll see there's a man in the middle who's viewing these things and saying them without qualifying them, just as he feels them. I try to keep in touch with the life around me. That's why I try to live inside this community in Connecticut; I take part in the meetings about highways, I follow people who are sick here, or changing their lives. And I keep in touch through my kids too; they are a great blessing to me. Two of them are living in a sort of counter-culture, so I follow their adventures with their friends, and what they do. It's necessary for me, every once in a while, to get out of this terrific concentration of my own pain and my own struggle, and say: 'Here's what's happening.' I've done that all the time. I've swung out.

*The Arrangement* was in the first person, *The Assassins* is in the third person. Actually, I'm everybody in it, and I try to like them all in a cruel and tough way, not in the way of 'Oh, everybody's nice!' There's a wonderful old man who's reactionary, and I'm like that – I have a conservative element. There are things in the tradition of America that I like very much, and that I think are being lost in the general petty hedonism of today. I like that austere, conservative, so-called reactionary element. But I'm also the kids. Though I don't like all the values of the hippies like their indolence and their passivity I feel very much like young people do today, that we should return to something that's basically simple and worthwhile. I reject, as they do, the goals of money-accumulation, prestige, and status-seeking.

The fact is that, like Cesario Flores in *The Assassins*, I was born in another country, and I have been in many other countries and therefore, more than most American men I know, I appreciate and value what we have here, while at the same time not closing my eyes to our faults and difficulties. I love this country, but I get very worried about it, as one might when a son or daughter is ill. When I see things going wrong I get concerned, and since I am an active person the concern causes activity. This place is too precious to me for me to be silent. Obviously the first duty of a citizen in a democracy is to speak his mind the best way he can and to exert his pressure on the state as strongly as he can.

There is also something perverse in my nature. I am happy when a number of people are angry at me. And happier when they are angry, but still, in spite of themselves, a little admiring. That means I have touched them under the skin, at the place I was aiming.

*Most artists start with autobiographical works but you ended up with them. What problems did this evolution raise?*

There is one piece of advice I give myself: 'When you are working, watch out for the elements and the scenes that you shy away from, even for those it embarrasses you to confront. The scene you're instinctively avoiding, the elements you most want to conceal, they are the most true and dramatic ones and the richest vein for you to dig into.'

The subjective problem of the artist is to stay in touch with himself. Don't censor your feelings, especially your unexpected, errant, destructive ones, your desires, legal or illegal, your rages, your disgusts, your foolishness, whatever embarrasses you most, whatever the censor within you tries to reject. Admit these to awareness; don't turn them off, embrace them. These things which you try to smooth out, turn off, reject, silence, erase, which embarrass you, are the most precious and most useful in art. The other thing I have to remember is 'More is not better!' and that power in a dramatic work, like an engine, comes from compression.

*You've always liked to work with a homogeneous group.*

Ideally, what should happen in every film is a complete unit. That's another thing I do; I've always used certain people – Karl Malden, Pat Hingle, Marlon Brando, Julie Harris, Lee Remick, Eli Wallach, Burl Ives, Kim Hunter, Jo Van Fleet, Paul Mann, Mike Strong, in film after film and play after play. I know them, I understand their limitations, and they trust me. I think basically they're honest, simple people without glamour. The men are not trying to show off how strong they are and the girls how pretty they are and all that nonsense. They're there to play human beings. It's the same with composers; I use the same composers over and over. The best way would be if they'd write the music while I was shooting the picture, if they watched rehearsals, met the actors, and not only read the script but knew how it was being directed and how it was being performed – if they hung around with me. That's the way I'd like it.

I used the same costume-designer in 85% of my films, a woman named Anna Hill Johnstone, who is one of the greatest collaborators I've ever had, in the sense that she completely tunes herself to me; she's so honest that there's never any sense in her costumes that she's trying to make a striking effect of her own, or get notices. The costumes and the scenery should not be noticed. The totality should be noticed – but not the direction, or the performances, or anything else. Anyway, Anna Hill Johnstone is the essence of that. For a film of a 'low order' like *Waterfront* or *America America*, she goes to the Salvation Army and gets all these old clothes that these bums leave there. She buys forty, fifty dresses of this kind and has them fumigated. In *On the Waterfront* she threw them on the floor and had the actors come in, and they picked what fitted them. The clothes all looked like they'd been worn. But when we made *The Arrangement*, I wanted an apron for Deborah Kerr and it cost 350 dollars! The worst of it was that when it was on her, it didn't look as if she'd picked it herself and used it many times, or washed it.

*What do you think are the most important stages in film-making?*

George Stevens said a film was one-third writing and preparation, one-third shooting, and one-third editing and scoring. That makes a lot of sense but it's never been the way I really felt. For me a film is half conceptual, the core of it – you get into what the events mean, what you're trying to express. I feel that that's the most important stage in a film. Then you work out the rest – it's just work. But if you are careless with the first stage, you make something which is flaccid at its centre. I like the audience to feel something is being said to them. I like them to be puzzled and disturbed.

Eisenstein had an idea of the tension in a shot which I always remembered. He gave an example of a pile of wood, and a man sitting with an axe in his hand. The man was not active, and the wood was waiting to be cut. There was a tension in that: you'd say, why isn't he cutting it? When is he going to cut it? Is it too much for him? And so on. The shot itself had a tension, a conflict in it. That's conception too. It isn't a matter of getting a shot of the pile of wood and a shot of the man; the whole thing is one shot. There was a time when I staged just like I do in the theatre, all medium-shot and people walking around. Hitchcock said scornfully of that kind of picture that it's just photographs of lips moving. He made fun of it. Later, when I began to study films, I saw his was a correct view. I began to cut and cut and cut. Well, now I do something in between. I try not to overstress now.

Many directors work with film more than I do in the way of

cutting. Though up to now I've been there every minute, though I know cutting is essential and central and a very creative process, I'm on top of it, but I don't do as much with it. George Stevens sits there himself and runs it back and forth, takes out this much here and adds that much there. Many old-time directors shoot more angles than I do, and then they make their picture in the cutting-room. I tend to make it more on the 'floor'. I'm very clear about what I want. I know it when I've got it, because I used to be an actor. I don't have a lot of set-ups, maybe seven or eight a day. I don't rely on miracles in the cutting-room. I shoot more economically now than I used to, with an idea of where the cuts should be. At the end of every day I tell the cutter the way I think it should go together. I say, you're free to experiment, but I want you to know my intention and try to work it out my way first.

My angles are plain, none of them are very tricky. When you have spectacular angles you notice them and not what's happening. There were a lot of cutters who influenced me, who taught me: Harmon Jones on *Panic*, David Weisbart on *Streetcar*, Dede Allen on *America America*, who is as good a cutter as there is. *The Visitors* was cut by a very sensitive man with excellent taste, who also photographed the picture, Nick Proferes. He's comparatively inexperienced, but very gifted. He cuts right to the heart of things.

*The theatre is increasingly foreign to you.*

I can't even read plays now. They don't seem to be in the rhythm of this time. Shakespeare is more contemporary than the plays that are being written today. He leaps from here to there, he goes to climaxes, and the figures are big-sized.

I am a person that moves. I think of life as moving – as a struggle, an escape, and a pursuit. Cinema is more compatible with this than the theatre. I have dreams, when I'm asleep, of working in the theatre again. I spent thirty-two years in the theatre, you know – but when I actually get up in the morning and I face life, I think of novels and films.

*The Rules of the Game* is the film which is the closest to my ideal on the screen. The highest form of art is when there's no formalistic 'genre' difference between the comedy, the farce, the tragedy, the social meaning, the symbolism. It's one piece. That's what I've been trying to do all my life, really. It's the way I view life. My films are not comedies, but there's a lot of fun in them; they're not tragedies, because there's a sense that life goes on, they don't collapse at the end in despair. *The Rules of the Game* has everything in it, but it's all one. Renoir is a big enough man so that he finds people at once tragic, very funny, ridiculous, beautiful, sensitive, insensitive, cruel, generous, foolish, heroic. And he uses nature a lot – the environment that we live in. He doesn't just move in front of scenery; he lives *in* an environment which is putting its imprint, its impression and its force on him. And I believe in that too.

*You never did a genre film, a Western, a musical, or a war film. Were you ever attracted by them?*

You must have the impression by now, as everybody in the moving picture community has, that I'm a terribly stubborn and unbending man. True, I'm not catholic in my tastes, I'm not a man of broad aesthetics. I only do the kind of work I like. I'm just not capable of doing the other thing. I'm not interested in it. I'm very self-centred and very narrow. People say: 'He makes the same pictures over and over again,' and this is said as a criticism, but I'm rather proud of it, I don't know whether a man has more than one or two statements to make in his life. I mean, it's like a spider – the same fluid comes out of me no matter what I do. I disguise it somewhat, I do; but I'm interested in things that have happened to *me*.

See, when I go out West, I'm thrilled by it, but I don't really know it. That's another thing I feel: that I'm making it up. I only made two pictures in Europe. One was *America America*, which I knew about. The only other picture was *Man on a Tightrope* and all through it I felt: I don't know anything about these people! I've never been attracted to forms *per se*. I've never said: 'Oh I must make a Western, I must make a musical.' It must be fun for other directors, but I don't give a damn about those films. I think of films as self-expression, as a way of saying whatever I feel: a cry of pain, a paean of praise, whatever thrills, whatever anger, whatever longing I've had in my life. It's just impossible for me to manufacture entertainment. I don't have any need of it, anyway, because one thing I've tried to do all my life is to keep my standard of living down, so that I'm never in a position to have to do anything for money. I don't have a chauffeur and big cars. That's why Barbara is nice, too, she's modest and moderate. We live simply, so I'm never forced to say: 'I *gotta* make —'.

177

My hopes are that I'll be able to say what's happened to me, what I've experienced and gone through – three or four more times. If I do that, then I'll be contented. I'm sixty-two now, so sometimes I feel I'd better hurry a little bit, because your memory begins to go at about seventy, and you don't remember in as much detail. But I'm in good shape and I never stop working. I never have a holiday, so to speak, from work, because that's all there is in life, to me. I'm working just as much when I'm on vacation as when I'm in the middle of things. One thing, no matter how irrelevant it may seem, is just as important as anything else in the bank of my memory. Also, I have an impatient temperament. Robert Anderson says I always like to fight out of a hole. And he says, if the hole is not there, I'd *dig* a hole so I could fight out of a hole! It's so much of a habit for me to have my back to the wall, and slug it out. Again and again, I had this experience of surmounting difficulties.

Part of my culture is that although I turned against the communists, I'm not actually against communism. I'm against Stalinism, that repressive kind of communism. Part of that culture was that 'escapism' was a dirty word. 'Commitment' was the good word. Kids say that everything that's not 'committed' is 'irrelevant'. And I still believe in it myself. But it seems to me there's a next step, which is, you just try to tell the truth. And if you try to tell the truth of what you see, the message is in there – you don't have to put it in. You don't conceal things from people or from yourself, you try to be accurate and objective and honest. You see things a certain way, anyway, but you have to tell *your* truth. I think I'm an 'essentialist', by which I mean I choose those realistic bits that contain some sort of essence, of an idea or a feeling. I don't have detail for its own sake, but I choose detail carefully because it has an essential meaning in relationship to the rest.

*In that sense your conception of 'commitment' in films has evolved too . . .*

I used to believe that commitment meant advocacy. But as I got older I wanted to eliminate all explanations and analyses. Just show the events. If an action doesn't tell it, an analysis won't convince. I think a dramatic story is best when it is conceived and written and developed so that it finally deals with the entire experience and with all aspects of the experience. A work of art should not show, it should not teach. It should be. Like a mountain or a cloud or a tree or any phenomenon of nature, different people looking at it should get different impressions. I like the following story. A judge is presiding at a trial. He is a very human and very fair old man. He listens carefully to the prosecuting attorney and at the end of the man's presentation, the judge is heard to murmur: 'You're right.' Then it is the turn of the defence attorney. The judge listens carefully, equally attentively. And at the end of this presentation, the judge is heard to murmur: 'You're right.' Now, sitting in the back of the room with his uncle is a little boy brought to watch his first trial. The little boy has heard what the judge said to himself and he was puzzled. And he says to his uncle, in a voice loud enough for the judge to hear: 'But they can't be both right!' And the judge heard the little boy across the court-room and he said to him: 'You're right.' And that is the end of the story. And that is dramaturgy.

Don't pretend to know the answer, but ask all the questions. A dilemma must truly be a dilemma, a situation apparently without a solution. The dilemma must be solved by 'life', but even when it is solved or 'finished', there must remain a doubt, a question in the mind of the reader or viewer. Did the right thing happen? Who knows?

In a work of the imagination, film or fiction, it is better to ask a question than make a statement. Let the reader or the viewer make the statement. Don't ever tell him, however indirectly, what he MUST think. The mood of bewilderment is the most honest and the most lifelike, therefore the most anxious. Instruction is an impertinence. Always leave an area of mystery. Don't answer the questions; ask them.

# Biofilmography

By Michel Ciment and Olivier Eyquem

Elia Kazan was born in Kadi-Keu in the suburbs of Istanbul on 7 September 1909 to George and Athena (Sismanoglou) Kazanjoglou. He spent his early childhood in Istanbul and Berlin, before moving with his family in 1913 to New York, where his father had established a rug business.

Kazan was educated at an elementary school in New York, at Mayfair School, New Rochelle High School (where he graduated in 1926), and Williams College (1930). He entered Yale University School of Drama in 1932, studied as an apprentice at the Group Theatre under Lee Strasberg and Harold Clurman in 1932–33, and was production assistant on John Howard Lawson's *The Pure in Heart*. He directed his first New York production in 1934, and followed this with several plays for the Group Theatre. After the dissolution of the Group Theatre (1941), Kazan moved to Hollywood, where he directed his first film in 1944, while continuing to pursue a successful stage career. In 1947 he founded the Actors' Studio with Cheryl Crawford and Robert Lewis. In 1950 he formed an independent production company, Newtown Productions, and – four years later – another company, Athena Enterprises, both based in New York. In 1960 he became director of the Repertory Theatre of Lincoln Center with Robert Whitehead, and staged its first production in 1964. Since 1962 Kazan has also written novels, two of which he has himself adapted and directed for the cinema.

Kazan married Molly Day Thatcher (1906–63) in 1932, and has four children: Judy (b. 1937), Chris (b. 1939, author of *The Visitors*), Nick (b. 1946), and Katy (b. 1948). He is presently married to Barbara Loden who, besides appearing in two of his films and playing the main part in the stage production of Arthur Miller's *After the Fall*, made her debut as a film director in 1971 with *Wanda*.

## Features

### A Tree Grows in Brooklyn (1945)

| | |
|---|---|
| Production Company | 20th Century-Fox |
| Producer | Louis D. Lighton |

| | |
|---|---|
| Director | Elia Kazan |
| Assistant Directors | Saul Wurtzel, Nicholas Ray |
| Script | Tess Slesinger, Frank Davis. Based on the novel by Betty Smith |
| Director of Photography | Leon Shamroy |
| Editor | Dorothy Spencer |
| Art Director | Lyle Wheeler |
| Set Decorators | Thomas Little, Frank E. Hughes |
| Special Effects | Fred Sersen |
| Music | Alfred Newman |
| Orchestrations | Edward B. Powell |
| Costumes | Bonnie Cashin |
| Sound | Bernard Freericks |

Dorothy McGuire (*Katie Nolan*), Joan Blondell (*Aunt Sissy*), James Dunn (*Johnny Nolan*), Lloyd Nolan (*McShane*), Peggy Ann Garner (*Francie Nolan*), Ted Donaldson (*Neeley Nolan*), James Gleason (*McGarrity*), Ruth Nelson (*Miss McDonough*), John Alexander (*Steve Edwards*), B. S. Pully (*Christmas Tree Vendor*), Ferike Boros (*Mrs Rommely*), J. Farrell MacDonald (*Carney*), Adeline DeWalt Reynolds (*Mrs Waters*), George Melford (*Mr Spencer*), Mae Marsh, Edna Jackson (*Tynmore Sisters*), Vincent Graeff (*Henny Gaddis*), Susan Lester (*Flossie Gaddis*), Johnny Berkes (*Mr Crackenbox*), Lillian Bronson (*Librarian*), Alec Craig (*Werner*), Charles Halton (*Mr Barker*), Al Bridge (*Cheap Charlie*), Joseph J. Green (*Hassler*), Virginia Brissac (*Miss Tilford*), Harry Harvey, Jr (*Herschel*), Art Smith (*Ice Man*), Norman Field, George Meader (*Principals of School*), Erskine Sanford (*Undertaker*), Martha Wentworth (*Mother*), Francis Pierlot (*Priest*), Al Eben (*Union Representative*), Peter Cusanelli (*Barber*), Robert Anderson (*Augie*), Harry Seymour (*Floor Walker*), Edith Hallor.

Filmed in 73 days. Released in USA, February 1945; GB, April 1945. Running time, 128 min.
Distributors: 20th Century-Fox.


## *Sea of Grass* (1947)

| | |
|---|---|
| Production Company | M-G-M |
| Producer | Pandro S. Berman |
| Director | Elia Kazan |
| 2nd Unit Director | James C. Havens |
| Assistant Director | Sid Sidman |
| Script | Marguerite Roberts, Vincent Lawrence. Based on the novel by Conrad Richter |
| Director of Photography | Harry Stradling |
| Editor | Robert J. Kern |
| Art Directors | Cedric Gibbons, Paul Groesse |
| Set Decorators | Edwin B. Willis, Mildred Griffiths |

| | |
|---|---|
| Special Effects | A. Arnold Gillespie, Warren Newcombe |
| Music | Herbert Stothart |
| Costumes | Walter Plunkett, Irene Valles |
| Sound | Douglas Shearer |

Spencer Tracy (*Jim Brewton*), Katharine Hepburn (*Lutie Cameron*), Melvyn Douglas (*Brice Chamberlain*), Robert Walker (*Brock Brewton*), Phyllis Thaxter (*Sarah Bess*), Edgar Buchanan (*Jeff*), Harry Carey (*Doc Reid*), Ruth Nelson (*Selena Hall*), William 'Bill' Phillips (*Banty*), Robert Armstrong (*Floyd McCurtin*), James Bell (*Sam Hall*), Robert Barrat (*Judge White*), Charles Trowbridge (*Cameron*), Russell Hicks (*Major Harney*), Trevor Bardette (*Andy*), Morris Ankrum (*Crane*), Nora Cecil (*Nurse*), Pat Henry (*Brock as a baby*), Duncan Richardson (*Brock at 3*), James Hawkins (*Brock at 5*), Norman Ollestead (*Brock at 8*), Carol Nugent, William Challee, Paul Langton.

Filmed in 75 days. Released in USA, April 1947; GB, January 1947. Running time, 131 min.
Distributors: M-G-M.

## *Boomerang!* (1947)

| | |
|---|---|
| Production Company | 20th Century-Fox |
| Executive Producer | Darryl F. Zanuck |
| Producer | Louis de Rochemont |
| Director | Elia Kazan |
| Assistant Director | Tom Dudley |
| Script | Richard Murphy. Based on a *Reader's Digest* article, 'The Perfect Case', by Anthony Abbott [Fulton Oursler] |
| Director of Photography | Norbert Brodine |
| Editor | Harmon Jones |
| Art Directors | Richard Day, Chester Gore |
| Set Decorators | Thomas Little, Phil D'Esco |
| Special Effects | Fred Sersen |
| Music | David Buttolph |
| Musical Director | Alfred Newman |
| Orchestrations | Edward B. Powell |
| Costumes | Kay Nelson |
| Wardrobe Director | Charles Le Maire |
| Sound | W. D. Flick, Roger Heman |

Dana Andrews (*Henry L. Harvey*), Jane Wyatt (*Mrs Harvey*), Lee J. Cobb (*Chief Robinson*), Cara Williams (*Irene Nelson*), Arthur Kennedy (*John Waldron*), Sam Levene (*Woods*), Taylor Holmes (*Wade*), Robert Keith (*McCreery*), Ed Begley (*Harris*), Leona Roberts (*Mrs Crossman*), Philip Coolidge (*Crossman*), Lester Lonergan (*Cary*), Lewis Leverett (*Whitney*), Richard Garrick (*Mr Rogers*), Karl

Malden (*Lieutenant White*), Ben Lackland (*James*), Helen Carew (*Annie*), Barry Kelley (*Sergeant Dugan*), Wyrley Birch (*Father Lambert*), Johnny Stearns (*Reverend Gardiner*), Guy Thomajan (*Cartucci*), Lucia Seger (*Mrs Lukash*), Dudley Sadler (*Dr Rainsford*), Walter Greaza (*Mayor Swayze*), Helen Hatch (*Miss Manion*), Joe Kazan (*Mr Lukash*), Ida McGuire (*Miss Roberts*), George Petrie (*O'Shea*), John Carmody (*Callahan*), Clay Clement (*Judge Tate*), E. J. Ballantine (*McDonald*), William Challee (*Stone*), Edgar Stehli (*Coroner*), Jimmy Dobson (*Bill*), Lawrence Paquin (*Sheriff*), Anthony Ross (*Warren*), Bert Freed (*Herron*), Royal Beal (*Johnson*), Bernard Hoffman (*Tom*), Fred Stewart (*Graham*), Lee Roberts (*Criminal*), Pauline Myers (*Girl*), Jacob Sandler (*Barman*), Herbert Rather (*Investigator*), Anna Minot (*Secretary*), Brian Keith (*Demonstrator*), Mayor Charles E. Moore, and the people of Stamford.

Locations filmed in Stamford, Connecticut. Filmed in 49 days. Released in USA, February 1947; GB, January 1947. Running time, 88 min.
Distributors: 20th Century-Fox.


## *Gentleman's Agreement* (1948)

| | |
|---|---|
| Production Company | 20th Century-Fox |
| Producer | Darryl F. Zanuck |
| Director | Elia Kazan |
| Assistant Director | Saul Wurtzel |
| Script | Moss Hart. Based on the novel by Laura Z. Hobson |
| Director of Photography | Arthur Miller |
| Editor | Harmon Jones |
| Art Directors | Lyle Wheeler, Mark-Lee Kirk |
| Set Decorators | Thomas Little, Paul S. Fox |
| Special Effects | Fred Sersen |
| Music | Alfred Newman |
| Orchestrations | Edward B. Powell |
| Costumes | Kay Nelson |
| Wardrobe Director | Charles Le Maire |
| Sound | Alfred Bruzlin, Roger Heman |

Gregory Peck (*Phil Green*), Dorothy McGuire (*Kathy*), John Garfield (*Dave Goldman*), Celeste Holm (*Anne*), Anne Revere (*Mrs Green*), June Havoc (*Miss Wales*), Albert Dekker (*John Minify*), Jane Wyatt (*Jane*), Dean Stockwell (*Tommy Green*), Nicholas Joy (*Dr Craigie*), Sam Jaffe (*Professor Lieberman*), Harold Vermilyea (*Jordan*), Ransom M. Sherman (*Bill Payson*), Roy Roberts (*Mr Calkins*), Kathleen Lockhart (*Mrs Minify*), Curt Conway (*Bert McAnny*), John Newland (*Bill*), Robert Warwick (*Weisman*), Louis Lorimer (*Miss Miller*), Howard Negley (*Tingler*), Victor Kilian (*Olsen*), Frank Wilcox (*Harry*), Marlyn Monk (*Receptionist*), Wilton Graff (*Maitre D*), Morgan Farley (*Clerk*), Robert Karnes,

Gene Nelson (*Ex-GIs*), Marion Marshall (*Guest*), Mauritz Hugo (*Columnist*), Jesse White (*Elevator Starter*), Olive Deering, Jane Green, Virginia Gregg, Helen Gerald.

Filmed in 65 days. Released in USA, March 1948; GB, June 1948. Running time, 118 min.
Distributors: 20th Century-Fox.


## *Pinky* (1949)

| | |
|---|---|
| Production Company | 20th Century-Fox |
| Producer | Darryl F. Zanuck |
| Production Manager | Joseph Behm |
| Director | Elia Kazan |
| Assistant Director | Wingate Smith |
| Script | Philip Dunne, Dudley Nichols. Based on the novel *Quality* by Cid Ricketts Sumner |
| Script Supervisor | Rose Steinberg |
| Director of Photography | Joe MacDonald |
| Camera Operator | Til Gabbani |
| Editor | Harmon Jones |
| Art Directors | Lyle Wheeler, J. Russell Spencer |
| Set Decorators | Thomas Little, Walter M. Scott |
| Special Effects | Fred Sersen |
| Music | Alfred Newman |
| Orchestrations | Edward B. Powell |
| Wardrobe Director | Charles Le Maire |
| Sound | Eugene Grossman, Roger Heman |

Jeanne Crain (*Pinky*), Ethel Barrymore (*Miss Em*), Ethel Waters (*Aunt Dicey*), William Lundigan (*Dr Thomas Adams*), Basil Ruysdael (*Judge Walker*), Kenny Washington (*Dr Canady*), Nina Mae McKinney (*Rozelia*), Griff Barnett (*Dr Joe*), Frederick O'Neal (*Jake Walters*), Evelyn Varden (*Melba Wooley*), Raymond Greenleaf (*Judge Shoreham*), Dan Riss (*Stanley*), Arthur Hunnicutt (*Police Chief*), William Hansen (*Mr Goolby*), Everett Glass (*Mr Wooley*), Bert Conway (*Loafer*), Harry Tenbrook (*Townsman*), Robert Osterloh (*Police Officer*), Jean Inness (*Saleslady*), Shelby Bacon (*Boy*), René Beard (*Teejore*), Tonya Overstreet, Juanita Moore (*Nurses*), Herbert Heywood, Paul Brinegar.

Kazan replaced John Ford after a few days' shooting.
Filmed in 52 days. Released in USA and GB, November 1949. Running time, 102 min.
Distributors: 20th Century-Fox.

## *Panic in the Streets* (1950)

| | |
|---|---|
| Production Company | 20th Century-Fox |
| Producer | Sol C. Siegel |
| Production Manager | Joseph Behm |
| Director | Elia Kazan |
| Assistant Director | Forrest E. Johnston |
| Script | Richard Murphy. Based on a story by Edna and Edward Anhalt |
| Adaptation | Daniel Fuchs |
| Script Supervisor | Stanley Scheuer |
| Director of Photography | Joe MacDonald |
| Camera Operator | Til Gabbani |
| Editor | Harmon Jones |
| Art Directors | Lyle Wheeler, Maurice Ransford |
| Set Decorators | Thomas Little, Fred J. Rode |
| Special Effects | Fred Sersen |
| Music | Alfred Newman |
| Orchestrations | Edward B. Powell, Herbert Spencer |
| Costumes | Travilla |
| Wardrobe Director | Charles Le Maire |
| Sound | W. D. Flick, Roger Heman |

Richard Widmark (*Dr Clinton Reed*), Paul Douglas (*Police Captain Warren*), Barbara Bel Geddes (*Nancy Reed*), Walter Jack Palance (*Blackie*), Zero Mostel (*Raymond Fitch*), Dan Riss (*Neff*), Alexis Minotis (*John Mefaris*), Guy Thomajan (*Poldi*), Tommy Cook (*Vince*), Edward Kennedy (*Jordan*), H. T. Tsiang (*Cook*), Lewis Charles (*Kochak*), Ray Muller (*Dubin*), Tommy Rettig (*Tom Reed*), Lenka Peterson (*Jeanette*), Pat Walshe (*Pat*), Paul Hostetler (*Dr Gafney*), George Ehmig (*Kleber*), John Schilleci (*Lee*), Waldo Pitkin (*Ben*), Leo Zinser (*Sergeant Phelps*), Beverly C. Brown (*Dr Mackey*), William A. Dean (*Cortelyou*), H. Waller Fowler, Jr (*Major Murray*), Red Moad (*Wynant*), Val Winter (*Commissioner Quinn*), Wilson Bourg, Jr (*Charlie*), Irving Vidacovich (*Johnston*), Mary Liswood (*Mrs Fitch*), Aline Stevens (*Rita*), Ruth Moore Mathews (*Mrs Dubin*), Stanley J. Reyes (*Redfield*), Darwin Greenfield (*Violet*), Emile Meyer (*Beauclyde*), Herman Cottman (*Scott*), Al Theriot (*Al*), Juan Villasana (*Hotel Proprietor*), Robert Dorsen (*Coast Guard Lieutenant*), Henry Marmet (*Anson*), Arthur Tong (*Lascar Boy*), Tiger Joe Marsh (*Bosun*).

Working titles: *Port of Entry* and *Outbreak*.
Released in USA, September 1950; GB, July 1950. Running time, 96 min.
Distributors: 20th Century-Fox.

## A Streetcar Named Desire (1951)

| | |
|---|---|
| Production Company | Group Productions |
| Producer | Charles K. Feldman |
| Production Manager | Norman Cook |
| Director | Elia Kazan |
| Assistant Director | Don Page |
| Script | Tennessee Williams. Based on his own play |
| Adaptation | Oscar Saul |
| Director of Photography | Harry Stradling |
| Editor | David Weisbart |
| Art Director | Richard Day |
| Set Decorator | George James Hopkins |
| Music | Alex North |
| Musical Director | Ray Heindorf |
| Costumes | Lucinda Ballard |
| Sound | C. A. Riggs |

Vivien Leigh (*Blanche DuBois*), Marlon Brando (*Stanley Kowalski*), Kim Hunter (*Stella Kowalski*), Karl Malden (*Mitch*), Rudy Bond (*Steve*), Nick Dennis (*Pablo*), Peg Hillias (*Eunice*), Wright King (*A Collector*), Richard Garrick (*Doctor*), Ann Dere (*The Matron*), Edna Thomas (*Mexican Woman*), Mickey Kuhn (*Sailor*), Chester Jones (*Street Vendor*), Marietta Canty (*Negro woman*), Maxie Thrower (*Passer-by*), Lyle Latell (*Policeman*), Mel Archer (*Foreman*), Charles Wagenheim (*Passer-by*).

Released in USA, March 1952; GB, February 1952. Running time, 122 min. Distributors: Warner Bros.


## Viva Zapata! (1952)

| | |
|---|---|
| Production Company | 20th Century-Fox |
| Producer | Darryl F. Zanuck |
| Director | Elia Kazan |
| Script | John Steinbeck |
| Director of Photography | Joe MacDonald |
| Editor | Barbara McLean |
| Art Directors | Lyle Wheeler, Leland Fuller |
| Set Decorators | Thomas Little, Claude Carpenter |
| Special Effects | Fred Sersen |
| Set Decorators | Thomas Little, Claude Carpenter |
| Special Effects | Fred Sersen |
| Music | Alex North |
| Musical Director | Alfred Newman |
| Orchestrations | Maurice de Packh |
| Costumes | Travilla |
| Wardrobe Director | Charles Le Maire |
| Sound | W. D. Flick, Roger Heman |

Marlon Brando (*Emiliano Zapata*), Jean Peters (*Josefa*), Antony Quinn (*Eufemio*), Joseph Wiseman (*Fernando*), Arnold Moss (*Don Nacio*), Alan Reed (*Pancho Villa*), Margo (*Soldadera*), Harold Gordon (*Madero*), Lou Gilbert (*Pablo*), Mildred Dunnock (*Señora Espejo*), Frank Silvera (*Huerta*), Nina Varela (*Aunt*), Florenz Ames (*Señor Espejo*), Bernie Gozier (*Zapatista*), Frank De Kova (*Colonel Guajardo*), Joseph Granby (*General Fuentes*), Pedro Regas (*Innocente*), Richard Garrick (*Old General*), Fay Roope (*Diaz*), Harry Kingston (*Don Garcia*), Ross Bagdasarian (*Officer*), Leonard George (*Husband*), Will Kuluva (*Lazaro*), Fernanda Elizcu (*Fuentes' Wife*), Abner Biberman (*Captain*), Philip Van Zandt (*Commanding Officer*), Lisa Fusaro (*Garcia's Wife*), Belle Mitchell (*Nacio's Wife*), Henry Silva (*Hernandez*), Ric Roman (*Overseer*), George J. Lewis (*Rurale*), Salvador Baguez, Peter Mamakos (*Soldiers*), Henry Corden (*Senior Officer*), Nestor Paiva (*New General*), Robert Filmer (*Capt. of Rurales*), Julia Montoya (*Wife*), Danny Nunez.

Kazan started to work on the script in 1943. Working titles: *The Little Tiger*, *The Angry Earth*, *Door to a Nation*, *The Invader*, and *Sudden Death*.
Released in USA and GB, March 1952. Running time, 113 min.
Distributors: 20th Century-Fox.


## *Man on a Tightrope* (1953)

| | |
|---|---|
| Production Company | 20th Century-Fox |
| Producer | Robert L. Jacks |
| Associate Producer | Gerd Oswald |
| Director | Elia Kazan |
| Assistant Director | Hans Tost |
| Script | Robert Sherwood. Based on the story *International Incident* by Neil Paterson |
| Director of Photography | Georg Krause |
| Editor | Dorothy Spencer |
| Art Directors | Hans H. Kuhnert, Theo Zwirsky |
| Musical Director | Franz Waxman |
| Orchestrations | Earle Hagen |
| Songs | Bert Reisfeld |
| Costumes | Ursula Maes |
| Wardrobe Director | Charles Le Maire |
| Sound | Martin Mueller, Karl Becker, Roger Heman |

Fredric March (*Karel Cernik*), Terry Moore (*Tereza Cernik*), Gloria Grahame (*Zama Cernik*), Cameron Mitchell (*Joe Vosdek*), Adolphe Menjou (*Fesker*), Robert Beatty (*Barovik*), Alex D'Arcy (*Rudolph*), Richard Boone (*Krofta*), Pat Henning (*Konradin*), Paul Hartman (*Jaromir*), John Dehner (*The Chief*), Dorothea Wieck (*Duchess*), Philip Kenneally (*The Sergeant*), Edelweiss Malchin (*Vina Konradin*), William Costello (*Captain*), Margaret Slezak (*Mrs Jaromir*), Hansi (*Kalka, the midget*), The Brumbach Circus (*The Cernik Circus*), Gert Froebe (*Plainclothes*

*Policeman*), Peter Beauvais (*SNB Captain*), Robert Charlebois (*SNB Lieutenant*), Rolf Naukhoff (*Police Agent*).

Locations filmed in Germany. Released in USA and GB, May 1953. Running time, 105 min.
Distributors: 20th Century-Fox.


## *On the Waterfront* (1954)

| | |
|---|---|
| Production Company | Horizon |
| Producer | Sam Spiegel |
| Assistant to Producer | Sam Rheiner |
| Director | Elia Kazan |
| Assistant Director | Charles H. Maguire |
| Script | Budd Schulberg. Based on articles by Malcolm Johnson |
| Director of Photography | Boris Kaufman |
| Editor | Gene Milford |
| Art Director | Richard Day |
| Music | Leonard Bernstein |
| Costumes | Anna Hill Johnstone |
| Sound | James Shields |

Marlon Brando (*Terry Malloy*), Eva Marie Saint (*Edie Doyle*), Karl Malden (*Father Barry*), Lee J. Cobb (*Johnny Friendly*), Rod Steiger (*Charley Malloy*), Pat Henning (*'Kayo' Dugan*), Leif Erickson (*Glover*), James Westerfield (*Big Mac*), John Heldabrand (*Mutt*), Rudy Bond (*Moose*), John Hamilton (*'Pop' Doyle*), Barry Macollum (*J.P.*), Don Blackman (*Luke*), Arthur Keegan (*Jimmy*), Mike O'Dowd (*Specs*), Martin Balsam (*Gillette*), Tony Galento (*Truck*), Tami Mauriello (*Tillio*), Fred Gwynne (*Slim*), Abe Simon (*Barney*), Joyce Lear (*Bad Girl*), Thomas Hanley (*Tommy*), Anne Hegira (*Mrs Collins*), Nehemiah Persoff (*Driver*), Pat Hingle (*Waiter*), Rebecca Sands (*Police Stenographer*), Tiger Joe Marsh, Pete King, Neil Hines (*Policemen*), Vince Barbi, Lilian Herlein, Donnell O'Brien, Clifton James, Michael Vincente Gazzo.

Kazan started work on the project in 1951. Working titles: *The Bottom of the River*, *Golden Warriors*, and *Crime on the Waterfront*.
Released in USA, October 1954; GB, September 1954. Running time, 108 min.
Distributors: Columbia.


## *East of Eden* (1955)

| | |
|---|---|
| Production Company | Warner Bros. |
| Producer | Elia Kazan |
| Director | Elia Kazan |

| Assistant Directors | Don Page, Horace Hough |
| Script | Paul Osborn. Based on the novel by John Steinbeck |
| Dialogue Director | Guy Thomajan |
| Director of Photography | Ted McCord (CinemaScope) |
| Colour Process | Warnercolor |
| Editor | Owen Marks |
| Art Directors | James Basevi, Malcolm Bert |
| Set Decorator | George James Hopkins |
| Music/Musical Director | Leonard Rosenman |
| Costumes | Anna Hill Johnstone |
| Sound | Stanley Jones |

Julie Harris (*Abra*), James Dean (*Cal Trask*), Raymond Massey (*Adam Trask*), Richard Davalos (*Aron Trask*), Burl Ives (*Sam, the Sheriff*), Jo Van Fleet (*Kate*), Albert Dekker (*Will Hamilton*), Lois Smith (*Ann*), Timothy Carey (*Joe*), Mario Siletti (*Piscora*), Lonny Chapman (*Roy*), Nick Dennis (*Rantani*), Harold Gordon (*Mr Albrecht*), Jonathan Haze (*Piscora's son*), Barbara Baxley (*Nurse*), Bette Treadville (*Madame*), Tex Mooney (*Bartender*), Harry Cording (*Bouncer*), Loretta Rush (*Card Dealer*), Bill Phillips (*Coalman*), Jack Carr, Roger Creed, Effie Laird, Wheaton Chambers, Ed Clark, Al Ferguson, Franklyn Farnum, Rose Plummer (*Carnival People*), John George (*Photographer*), Earle Hodgins (*Shooting Gallery Attendant*), C. Ramsay Hill (*English Officer*), Edward McNally (*Soldier*), Jack Henderson, Ruth Gillis, Joe Greene, Mabel and June Smaney.

Released in USA, April 1955; GB, July 1955. Running time, 115 min.
Distributors: Warner Bros.

## *Baby Doll* (1956)

| Production Company | Newtown Productions |
| Producer | Elia Kazan |
| Production Manager | Forrest E. Johnston |
| Director | Elia Kazan |
| Assistant Director | Charles H. Maguire |
| Script | Tennessee Williams. Based on his one-act plays *27 Wagons Full of Cotton* and *The Unsatisfactory Supper* or *The Long Stay Cut Short* |
| Director of Photography | Boris Kaufman |
| Editor | Gene Milford |
| Art Director | Richard Sylbert |
| Associate Art Director | Paul Sylbert |
| Music | Kenyon Hopkins |
| Costumes | Anna Hill Johnstone |
| Wardrobe | Flo Transfield |
| Speech Consultant | Marguerite Lamkin |
| Sound | Edward J. Johnstone |

Carroll Baker (*Baby Doll Meighan*), Karl Malden (*Archie Lee Meighan*), Eli Wallach (*Silva Vacarro*), Mildred Dunnock (*Aunt Rose*), Lonny Chapman (*Rock*), Eades Hogue (*Town Marshal*), Noah Williamson (*Deputy*), Jimmy Williams (*Mayor*), John Stuart Dudley (*Doctor*), Madeleine Sherwood (*Nurse*), Will Lester (*Sheriff*), Rip Torn (*Brick*), and the people of Benoit, Mississippi.

Kazan started work on the script (which was originally based on two other plays by Williams, *The Last of the Solid Gold Watches* and *This Property is Condemned*) in 1952. Working titles: *Hide and Seek*, *The Whip Master*, and *Mississippi Woman*. Released in USA and GB, December 1956. Running time, 114 min. Distributors: Warner Bros.


## *A Face in the Crowd* (1957)

| | |
|---|---|
| Production Company | Newtown Productions |
| Producer | Elia Kazan |
| Production Manager | George Justin |
| Director | Elia Kazan |
| Assistant Director | Charles H. Maguire |
| Script | Budd Schulberg. Based on his short story *Your Arkansas Traveller* from his book *Some Faces in the Crowd* |
| Director of Photography | Harry Stradling |
| Associate Director of Photography | Gayne Rescher |
| Camera Operators | Saul Midwall, James Fitzsimons |
| Editor | Gene Milford |
| Art Directors | Richard Sylbert, Paul Sylbert |
| Music | Tom Glazer |
| Songs: | |
| 'A Face in the Crowd' | |
| 'Free Man in the Morning' | |
| 'Mama Guitar' | |
| 'Vitajex Jingle' | Tom Glazer, Budd Schulberg |
| Costumes | Anna Hill Johnstone |
| Wardrobe | Flo Transfield |
| Sound Editor | Don Olson |
| Sound | Ernest Zatorsky |
| Technical Advisers | Charles Irving, Toby Bruce |

Andy Griffith (*Lonesome Rhodes*), Patricia Neal (*Marcia Jeffries*), Anthony Franciosa (*Joey Kieley*), Walter Matthau (*Mel Miller*), Lee Remick (*Betty Lou Fleckum*), Percy Waram (*Colonel Hollister*), Rod Brasfield (*Beanie*), Charles Irving (*Mr Luffler*), Howard Smith (*J. B. Jeffries*), Paul McGrath (*Macey*), Kay Medford (*1st Mrs Rhodes*), Alexander Kirkland (*Jim Collier*), Marshall Neilan (*Senator Fuller*), Big Jeff Bess (*Sheriff Hesmer*), Henry Sharp (*Abe Steiner*), Willie Feibel,

Larry Casazza (*Printers*), P. Jay Sidney (*Llewellyn*), Eva Vaughan (*Mrs Cooley*), Burl Ives (*Himself*), Bennet Cerf, Betty Furness, Faye Emerson, Virginia Graham, Sam Levenson, Mike Wallace (*Extras in bar sequence*), Logan Ramsey (*TV Director*), Earl Wilson, Walter Winchell, Vera Walton, John Stuart Dudley, Fred Stewart, Rip Torn, Granny Sense, Harold Jinks, Diana Sands, Charles Nelson Reilly, Sandy Wirth.

Locations filmed in Arkansas, August 1956, and in Memphis and New York. Released in USA, June 1957; GB, October 1957. Running time, 126 min. Distributors: Warner Bros.

## *Wild River* (1960)

| | |
|---|---|
| Production Company | 20th Century-Fox |
| Producer | Elia Kazan |
| Director | Elia Kazan |
| Assistant Director | Charles Maguire |
| Script | Paul Osborn. Based on the novels *Mud on the Stars* by William Bradford Huie and *Dunbar's Cove* by Borden Deal |
| Director of Photography | Ellsworth Fredericks (CinemaScope) |
| Colour Process | De Luxe Color |
| Colour Consultant | Leonard Doss |
| Editor | William Reynolds |
| Art Directors | Lyle R. Wheeler, Herman A. Blumenthal |
| Set Decorators | Walter M. Scott, Joseph Kish |
| Music | Kenyon Hopkins |
| Costumes | Anna Hill Johnstone |
| Sound | Eugene Grossman, Richard Vorisek |

Montgomery Clift (*Chuck Glover*), Lee Remick (*Carol Garth*), Jo Van Fleet (*Ella Garth*), Albert Salmi (*Hank Bailey*), Jay C. Flippen (*Hamilton Garth*), James Westerfield (*Cal Garth*), Barbara Loden (*Betty Jackson*), Frank Overton (*Walter Clark*), Malcolm Atterbury (*Sy Moore*), Robert Earl Jones (*Ben*), Bruce Dern (*Jack Roper*), James Steakley (*Mayor*), Hardwick Stewart (*Marshal Hogue*), Big Jeff Bess (*Joe John*), Judy Harris (*Barbara-Ann*), Jim Menard (*Jim Junior*), Patricia Perry (*Mattie*), John Dudley (*Todd*), Alfred E. Smith (*Thompson*), Mark Menson (*Winters*), Pat Hingle (*Narrator*).

Kazan started work on the film in 1955. After finishing a first script called *Garth Island*, he asked for the contribution of Ben Maddow and Calder Willingham. Nine different versions of the script were worked out while the film went through the following titles: *Time and Tide*, *God's Valley*, *As the River Rises*, *The Swift Season*, *The Coming of Spring*, and *New Face in the Valley*.
Released in USA, June 1960; GB, July 1960. Running time, 109 min.
Distributors: 20th Century-Fox.

## *Splendor in the Grass* (1961)

| | |
|---|---|
| Production Company | Newtown Productions/NBI |
| Producer | Elia Kazan |
| Associate Producers | William Inge, Charles H. Maguire |
| Director | Elia Kazan |
| Assistant Directors | Don Kranze, Ulu Grosbard (New York scenes) |
| Script | William Inge |
| Script Supervisor | Marguerite James |
| Director of Photography | Boris Kaufman |
| Colour Process | Technicolor |
| Editor | Gene Milford |
| Production Designer | Richard Sylbert |
| Set Decorator | Gene Callahan |
| Music/Musical Director | David Amram |
| Costumes | Anna Hill Johnstone |
| Wardrobe | Florence Transfield, George Newman |
| Choreography | George Tapps |
| Sound | Edward Johnstone |

Natalie Wood (*Wilma Dean Loomis*), Warren Beatty (*Bud Stamper*), Pat Hingle (*Ace Stamper*), Audrey Christie (*Mrs Loomis*), Barbara Loden (*Ginny Stamper*), Zohra Lampert (*Angelina*), Fred Stewart (*Del Loomis*), Joanna Roos (*Mrs Stamper*), Jan Norris (*Juanita Howard*), Gary Lockwood (*Toots*), Sandy Dennis (*Kay*), Crystal Field (*Hazel*), Marla Adams (*June*), Lynn Loring (*Carolyn*), John McGovern (*Doc Smiley*), Martine Bartlett (*Miss Metcalf*), Sean Garrison (*Glenn*), William Inge (*Reverend Whiteman*), Charles Robinson (*Johnny Masterson*), Phyllis Diller (*Texas Guinan*), Buster Bailey (*Old Man at Country Club*), Jake La Motta (*Waiter*), Billy Graham, Charlie Norkus (*Young men at party*), Lou Antonio (*Roustabout*), Adelaide Klein (*Italian Mother*), Phoebe Mackay (*Maid*), Mark Slade, Marjorie J. Nichols, Richard Abbott, Patricia Ripley.

Released in USA, October 1961; GB, January 1962. Running time, 124 min.
Distributors: Warner Bros.

## *America America* [British title: *The Anatolian Smile*] (1963)

| | |
|---|---|
| Production Company | Warner Bros. |
| Producer | Elia Kazan |
| Associate Producer | Charles H. Maguire |
| Production Assistant | Burtt Harris |
| Director | Elia Kazan |
| Script | Elia Kazan. Based on his own novel and his unpublished story *Hamal* |
| Script Supervisor | Marie Kenney |
| Director of Photography | Haskell Wexler |

| | |
|---|---|
| Camera Operator | Harlowe Stengel |
| Optical Effects | Film Opticals Inc. |
| Editor | Dede Allen |
| Production Designer | Gene Callahan |
| Music | Manos Hadjidakis |
| Lyrics | Nikos Gatsos |
| Costumes | Anna Hill Johnstone |
| Sound Editor | Edward Beyer |
| Sound | L. Robbins, Richard Vorisek |

Stathis Giallelis (*Stavros Topouzoglou*), Frank Wolff (*Vartan Damadian*), Harry Davis (*Isaac Topouzoglou*), Elena Karam (*Vasso Topouzoglou*), Estelle Hemsley (*Grandmother Topouzoglou*), Gregory Rozakis (*Hohanness Gardashian*), Lou Antonio (*Abdul*), Salem Ludwig (*Odysseus Topouzoglou*), John Marley (*Garabet*), Johanna Frank (*Vartuhi*), Linda Marsh (*Thomna Sinnikoglou*), Paul Mann (*Aleko Sinnikoglou*), Robert H. Harris (*Aratoon Kebabian*), Katharine Balfour (*Sophia Kebabian*), Dimitris Nicolaides, Leonard George, Gina Trikonis, George Stefans, Peter Dawson, Xander Chello, Carl Low.

Filmed at the Alfa Studios, Athens. Released in USA, December 1963; GB, April 1964. Running time, 168 min.
Distributors: Warner Bros.

## *The Arrangement* (1969)

| | |
|---|---|
| Production Company | Athena Enterprises |
| Producer | Elia Kazan |
| Associate Producer | Charles H. Maguire |
| Director | Elia Kazan |
| Assistant Director | Burtt Harris |
| Script | Elia Kazan. Based on his own novel |
| Director of Photography | Robert Surtees (Panavision) |
| Colour Process | Technicolor |
| Editor | Stefan Arnsten |
| Production Designer | Gene Callahan |
| Art Director | Malcolm Bert |
| Set Decorator | Audrey Blasdel |
| Music | David Amram |
| Costumes | Theodora Van Runkle |
| Sound Editor | Larry Jost |
| Sound | Richard Vorisek |

Kirk Douglas (*Eddie Anderson/Evangelos*), Faye Dunaway (*Gwen*), Deborah Kerr (*Florence Anderson*), Richard Boone (*Sam Anderson*), Hume Cronyn (*Arthur*), Michael Higgins (*Michael*), John Randolph Jones (*Charles*), Carol Rossen (*Gloria*),

Anne Hegira (*Thomna*), William Hansen (*Dr Weeks*), Charles Drake (*Finnegan*), Harold Gould (*Dr Liebman*), E. J. André (*Uncle Joe*), Michael Murphy (*Father Draddy*), Philip Bourneuf (*Judge Morris*), Diane Hull (*Ellen*), Barry Sullivan (*Chet Collier*), Ann Doran (*Nurse Costello*), Chet Stratton (*Charlie*), Paul Newlan (*Banker*), Steve Bond (*Eddie at 12*), Jim Halferty (*Eddie at 18*), Joseph Rogan/Joseph Cherry (*Gwen's baby*), Clint Kimbrough (*Ben*), Kirk Livesey, Bert Conway, John Lawrence, Elmer J. McGovern, Barry Russo, Dee Carroll, Richard Morrill, Betty Bresler, Virginia Peters, Pat Paterson, Dorothy Konrad, Maureen McCormick.

Released in USA, November 1969; GB, January 1970. Running time, 125 min. Distributors: Warner Bros.


## *The Visitors* (1971)

| | |
|---|---|
| Production Company | Chris Kazan–Nick Proferes Productions |
| Producers | Chris Kazan, Nick Proferes |
| Director | Elia Kazan |
| Script | Chris Kazan |
| Director of Photography | Nick Proferes (Super 16, colour) |
| Lighting | Michael Mannes |
| Assisted by | William Mamches |
| Editor | Nick Proferes |
| Music | Bach's Suite No. 1 for lute, played by William Matthews (guitar) |
| Sound Editor | Nina Shulman |
| Assistant Sound Editor | Marilyn Frauenglass |
| Sound | Dale Whitman |

Patrick McVey (*Harry Wayne*), Patricia Joyce (*Martha Wayne*), James Woods (*Bill Schmidt*), Chico Martinez (*Tony Rodriguez*), Steve Railsback (*Mike Nickerson*).

Shot on location in Elia Kazan's property in Newtown (Connecticut). Flashback scene shot in Westchester County (NY).
Working title: *Home Free*
Released in USA, February 1972. Not yet released in GB. Running time, 90 min.
Distributors: United Artists.

## Shorts

*People of the Cumberland* (1937)

| | |
|---|---|
| Production Company | Frontier Films |
| Director | Elia Kazan |
| Script | Elia Kazan |
| Director of Photography | Ralph Steiner |

Running time, 20 min.


## Film performances

1934  *Café Universal* and *Pie in the Sky* (both directed by Ralph Steiner)
1940  *City for Conquest* (as Googie. d: Anatole Litvak)
1941  *Blues in the Night* (as the clarinet player. d: Anatole Litvak)


## Theatre

Prior to his professional career, Kazan appeared in several plays at Yale, including: *Love of One's Neighbour* (as a Tourist), *Dr Faustus* by Christopher Marlowe (as Wagner), *The Stepmother* (as Dr Gardner), *Reckless* by Lynn Riggs, *Andromaque* by Jean Racine (as Pylade), *Thirty Minutes in a Street, Blood o' Kings, Merry-go-round* by Albert Maltz and George Sklar (as Joe Zelli), *I Got the Blues* (as Sam), *Until the Day I Die*, and *The Three Sisters* by Anton Chekhov (as Solyony).


## Stage performances

1932  *Chrysalis* by Rose Albert Porter (as Louis; also stage manager. Martin Beck Th., 15 November)
1933  *Men in White* by Sidney Kingsley (as the Orderly; also stage manager. Broadhurst Th., 26 September)
1934  *Gold Eagle Guy* by Melvin Levy (as Polyzoides; also stage manager. Morosco Th., 28 November)
1935  *Till the Day I Die* (as Baum) and *Waiting for Lefty* (as Agate Keller) by Clifford Odets (Longacre Th., 26 March)
      *Paradise Lost* by Clifford Odets (as Kewpie. Longacre Th., 9 December)
1936  *Johnny Johnson* by Paul Green (as Pte. Kearns. 44th Street Th., 19 November)
1937  *Golden Boy* by Clifford Odets (as Eddie Fuselli and Joe Bonaparte. Belasco Th., 4 November. Kazan toured in the same play during the 1938–39

season and also appeared in London in the role of Eddie Fuselli at the St James's Th., 21 June 1938)

1939 *The Gentle People* by Irwin Shaw (as Eli Lieber. Belasco Th., 5 January)

1940 *Night Music* by Clifford Odets (as Steve Takis. Broadhurst Th., 22 February)

*Liliom* by Ferenc Molnar (as Ficzur, the 'sparrow'. 44th Street Th., 25 March)

1941 *Five Alarm Waltz* by Lucille S. Prumbs (as Adam Boguris. Playhouse Th., 13 March)

## Stage productions

1931 *The Second Man* by S. N. Behrman (Toy Th., Atlantic City)

1934 *Dimitroff* by Elia Kazan and Art Smith (co-director: Art Smith. Group Th.)

1935 *The Young Go First* by Peter Martin, Charles Scudder and Charles Friedman (co-director: Alfred Saxe. Park Th., 28 May)

1936 *The Crime* by Michael Blankfort (co-director: Alfred Saxe)

1938 *Casey Jones* by Robert Ardrey (Fulton Th., 19 February)

1939 *Quiet City* by Irwin Shaw (Belasco Th., 16 April)

*Thunder Rock* by Robert Ardrey (Mansfield Th., 14 November)

1941 *It's Up To You* by Arthur Arent (Dept. of Agriculture)

1942 *Café Crown* by Hy S. Kraft (Cort Th., 23 January)

*The Strings, My Lord, are False* by Paul Vincent Carroll (Royale Th., 19 May)

*The Skin of Our Teeth* by Thornton Wilder (Plymouth Th., 18 November)

1943 *Harriet* by Florence Ryerson and Colin Clements (Henry Miller Th., 3 March)

*One Touch of Venus* by S. J. Perelman and Ogden Nash (Martin Beck Th., 14 March)

1944 *Jakobowsky and the Colonel* by S. N. Behrman (Martin Beck Th., 14 March)

*Swing out, Sweet Land* by Jean and Walter Kerr (International Th., 27 December)

1945 *Deep are the Roots* by Arnaud D'Usseau and James Gow (Fulton Th., 26 September)

*Dunnigan's Daughter* by S. N. Behrman (Golden Th., 26 December)

1947 *All My Sons* by Arthur Miller (Kazan also produced with Harold Clurman, Walter Fried and Herbert H. Harris. Coronet Th., 29 January)

*Truckline Café* by Maxwell Anderson (as producer only. Belasco Th., 27 February)

*A Streetcar Named Desire* by Tennessee Williams (Ethel Barrymore Th., 3 December)

1948 *Sundown Beach* by Bessie Breuer (Belasco Th., 7 September)

*Love Life* by Alan Jay Lerner (46th Street Th., 7 October)

1949 *Death of a Salesman* by Arthur Miller (Morosco Th., 10 February)

1952 *Flight into Egypt* by George Tabori (Music Box Th., 18 March)

1953   *Camino Real* by Tennessee Williams (National Th., 19 March)
       *Tea and Sympathy* by Robert Anderson (Ethel Barrymore Th., 30
       September)
1955   *Cat on a Hot Tin Roof* by Tennessee Williams (Morosco Th., 24 March)
1957   *The Dark at the Top of the Stairs* by William Inge (Kazan also produced
       with Saint Subber. Music Box Th., 5 December)
1958   *J.B.* by Archibald MacLeish (ANTA, 11 December)
1959   *Sweet Bird of Youth* by Tennessee Williams (Martin Beck Th., 10 March)
1964   *After the Fall* by Arthur Miller (ANTA Washington Square Th., 23
       January)
       *But for whom Charlie* by S. N. Behrman (ANTA Washington Square Th.,
       12 March)
       *The Changeling* by Thomas Middleton and William Rowley (ANTA
       Washington Square Th., December)

## Publications

Novels

*America America*, 1962
*The Arrangement*, 1967
*The Assassins*, 1971 (all published by Stein and Day, New York)

Articles, etc.

'The Director's Playbill', N.Y. *Herald Tribune*, September 1943
'Beginner's Notes' (diary on the shooting of *A Tree Grows in Brooklyn*, edited by
   Nicholas Ray [unpublished], 1944)
'Audience Tomorrow, preview in New Guinea', *Theater Arts*, October 1945
'Advertisement' (with Harold Clurman; on Maxwell Anderson's *Truckline Café*, 1
   March 1946)
'About Broadway and the Herring Catch', N.Y. *Times*, 16 October 1949
'Pressure Problem' (on the enforced cuts in *A Streetcar Named Desire*), N.Y. *Times*,
   October 1951
'A Statement', N.Y. *Times*, 4 December 1952
'Playwright's Letter to the World' (on *Camino Real*), 15 March 1953
'Movie that had to be made' (on *Man on a Tightrope*), 3 May 1953
'The Director's Notebook' (on *A Streetcar Named Desire*), in *The Griffin*, 1953
'A Star will find its Sky', 1957
'Paean of Praise for a Face above the Crowd' (on Budd Schulberg), May 1957
'The writer and motion pictures', *Sight and Sound*, Summer 1957
Preface to *Seen any Good Films Lately?* by William K. Zinsser, 1958
'Knowing Everything is only the Beginning', N.Y. *Herald Tribune*, 5 July 1961

'Theater: new stages, new plays, new actors' (on the Lincoln Center experiment), N.Y. *Times* Magazine, 23 September 1962
'Shooting America' (diary of the shooting of *America America*, unpublished), 1963
'Here's what's behind *America America*', *Valley Times*, 2 April 1964
'Kazan unbowed by year of repertory', Newark *Sunday News*, 2 August 1964
'On process development of repertory, or a team needs patience and years', N.Y. *Times*, 9 August 1964
'Political passion play act two' (on the Democrat Convention in Chicago), published in New York, 23 September 1968


## Interviews

With Lewis Gillenson, *Harper's Bazaar*, November 1951
John Durniat: 'Amateurs can be great', *Popular Photography*, May 1955
'A Quiz for Kazan', *Theater Arts*, No. 11, 1956
Frederic Morton: 'Gadge!', *Esquire*, February 1957
Ward Moorehouse: 'Keeping up with Kazan', *Theater Arts*, June 1957
'An interview with Elia Kazan', *Equity*, December 1957
Henri Rode: 'Entretien avec Elia Kazan', *Cinémonde*, August 1961
'Candid conversation: Elia Kazan', *Show Business Illustrated*, February 1962
Robin Bean: 'Elia Kazan on "The Young Agony" ', *Films and Filming*, March 1962
Jean Domarchi and André S. Labarthe: 'Entretien avec Elia Kazan', *Cahiers du Cinéma*, April 1962
Donald Stewart: 'An interview with Elia Kazan', *Nugget*, 1963
James F. Fixx: 'Who cares what the boss thinks?', *Saturday Review*, 28 December 1963
'Arthur Miller ad-libs on Elia Kazan', *Show*, January 1964
Richard Schechner and Theodore Hoffman: 'Look, there's the American theatre', *Tulane Drama Review*, Winter 1964
'Elia Kazan ad-libs on *The Changeling*', *Show*, January 1965
Michel Ciment and Roger Tailleur: 'Entretien avec Elia Kazan', *Positif*, October 1966
Michel Delahaye: 'Entretien avec Elia Kazan', *Cahiers du Cinéma*, November 1966
Claudine Tavernier: 'Entretien avec Elia Kazan', *Cinéma 70*, November 1970
Bernard R. Kantor, Irwin R. Blacker and Anne Kramer: 'Directors at work: interviews with American film-makers', 1970
Stuart Byron and Martin L. Rubin: 'Elia Kazan Interview', *Movie* no. 19, 1972
Charles Silver and Joel Zuker: 'Visiting Kazan', *Film Comment*, Summer 1972


## Short interviews

J. B. Bidgman, *The National Herald*, 4 April 1943
Murray Schumbach: 'A Director named Gadge', N.Y. *Times*, 1947
Ward Morehouse: 'Kazan demands truth in plays', 1956

'Kazan decries the James Dean Myth', *Mirror News*, 25 April 1957
Mike Wallace: 'What about movie censorship?', *Congressional Record*, 21 August
    1957
Ernest Schier: 'You can have Broadway', *Sunday Bulletin* (Philadelphia), 1 October
    1961
Henry T. Murdock: 'Elia Kazan splendid salesman for *Splendor*', *Philadelphia
    Inquirer*, 1 October 1961
John Bustin: 'Elia Kazan: adult moviemaker', *American Statesman*, 3 October 1961
Elinor Hughes: 'Kazan describes working with Inge on *Splendor*', *Boston Herald*, 6
    October 1961
Simone Anger, *La Presse* (Montreal), 9 October 1961
Paul Toupin: 'Le cinéma, je l'apprends de film en film', *Montreal Photo Journal*, 14
    October 1961
Interview in *Newsweek*, 16 October 1961
'Elia Kazan talks about his two lives', *Times*, 9 January 1962
George Christian: 'A chat with Kazan', Houston *Post*, 1 March 1964
Kaspar Monahan: 'Elia Kazan speaks his mind', Pittsburgh *Press*, 1 March 1964
George Oppenheimer: 'Kazan answers critics on *The Changeling*', *Daily Times*,
    Marmaroneck, 18 November 1964
'Elia Kazan le faiseur de rebelles', *Pariscope*, 12 January 1966
Guy Braucourt: 'Elia Kazan: *L'Arrangement* fait le procès de l'Amérique', *Lettres
    Françaises*, 8 April 1970
With Kira Appel, *France-Soir*, 8 April 1972
With Nicole Jolivet, *France-Soir*, 6 May 1972
With Guy Le Clech, *Le Figaro*, 10 June 1972

## Unpublished plays

*Bloody Ground*, melodrama in one act (date unknown)
*The Blood of the Brewsters* (June 1931)
*Skit Farce in one act by Elia Kazan* (June 1931)
*Triangle Seventeenth, a collegiate comedy* (June 1931)
*A Prodigee Genius*, one-act satire (November 1931)
*The Failure*, one-act drama (December 1931)
*Bridegroom* (1932)
*Saved* (1932)
*Alumni Day, a play in three acts* (1933)
Two strike plays (including *For Bread and Unity*, a class war fairy tale, 1933–34)
*College Days* (revised version of *Alumni Day*, 1937)
A play by Elia Kazan and Clifford Odets (title unknown)

## Radio

Elia Kazan appeared on the Philip Morris Hour, the Kate Smith Hour, and the
    Group Theatre radio programme.